Partisan or Neutral?

Partisan or Neutral?

The Futility of Public Political Theory

MICHAEL J. WHITE

ROWMAN & LITTLEFIELD PUBLISHERS, INC.
Lanham • New York • Boulder • Oxford

ROWMAN & LITTLEFIELD PUBLISHERS, INC.

Published in the United States of America
by Rowman & Littlefield Publishers, Inc.
4720 Boston Way, Lanham, Maryland 20706

12 Hid's Copse Road
Cummor Hill, Oxford OX 9JJ, England

Copyright © 1997 by Rowman & Littlefield Publishers, Inc.

British Library Cataloging in Publication Information Available

Library of Congress Cataloging-in-Publication Data

White, Michael J., 1948-
   Partisan or neutral : the futility of public political theory /
Michael J. White.
       p. cm. — (Studies in social, political, and legal philosophy)
       Includes bibliographical references and index.
       ISBN 0-8476-8453-9 (cloth : alk. paper). — ISBN 0-8476-8454-7
(pbk. : alk. paper)
       1. Political science—Philosophy. 2. Liberalism. I. Title.
II. Series.
JA71.W4558 1997
320.5—dc20   96-48980
                                                                  CIP

ISBN 0–8476–8453–9 (cloth : alk. paper)
ISBN 0–8476–8454–7 (pbk. : alk. paper)

Printed in the United States of America

Contents

Preface

There is, as the persistent reader will discover, more of the hedgehog than the fox to this book. Its *idée maîtresse* is the futility of a search for a public moral-political theory for contemporary, Western constitutional democracies. Such a theory is supposed to be a *moral-political* theory in that its primary aim is to justify or to legitimate, and thereby to stabilize and to entrench, not only a certain set of democratic political institutions and practices but also a set of generally liberal or semi-liberal political principles and attitudes. It is supposed to be *public* in the sense that any rational, reasonable, and decent citizen of a contemporary constitutional democracy should be able to endorse it, irrespective of that citizen's particular conception of the good, individual life-plan, or peculiar religious, moral, or philosophical commitments. The development of a political theory so conceived represents an attempt to 'stop History', in the sense of both (a) implying that the morally proper 'end' of the history of human political organization has been reached in the form of democratic political institutions and liberal moral-political principles and (b) assuming that such institutions and principles can be both perfected and more-or-less perpetually maintained by the appropriate justifying theory. My main point in response, to which I shall return perhaps too often, is that democratic political processes typically issue in acquiescences, compromises, agreements, and modi vivendi that are unsystematic, piecemeal, contingent, and revocable. Moreover, they are accepted (or acquiesced in) by the parties to democratic political processes for diverse reasons, often under differing circumstances, and with varying degrees of enthusiasm. By its very nature, a justifying or legitimating theory will appeal to a more unified and deeper set of principles and, in so doing, will usu-

ally represent some rather fundamental assumptions and attitudes about the individual and social aspects of human existence. Thus, this public process becomes a matter of attempting
to justify/legitimate the relatively less controversial (i.e., the
piecemeal and provisional results of actual democratic processes) by the relatively more controversial (i.e., a coherent moral-
political theory, to which the objections by dissidents may well
be more principled and deeply seated than are the objections
by dissidents to the *particular* political decisions that such a
theory is supposed to legitimate).

Of course, there is nothing surprising or amiss about the
'deeper principles' of a theory being logically stronger and perhaps more controversial than the 'theorems' or more particular
conclusions of the theory in question. But this situation becomes
deeply problematic when the theory in question is supposed
to be public in the sense that I have just indicated and when
the phenomena the theory is to justify/legitimate are the concrete output of the democratic processes of compromise and acquiescence. I shall maintain—in the terms of the title of this
book—that any attempt to construct a public justifying/
legitimating political theory will prove to be, not neutral, but
partisan in the same sense as political theories that are avow-
edly so. Thus the subtitle "The Futility of Public Political Theory," where the phrase "public political theory" bears its usual
connotation of a political justifying/legitimating theory that is
supposed to be neutral in a sense that is antithetical to 'partisan'. Much of the content of this book is an anatomy, historical
and conceptual, of liberalism as a modern *fons et origo* of this
conception of political theory as neutral and nonpartisan. In
chapter 4 I draw a connection between the search, on the part
of many contemporary theorists of political liberalism, for a
public justifying theory and the residual commitment by such
theorists to two other ideas: (a) the idea that contemporary
Western constitutional democracies can and should, to some
degree, instantiate the notion of a 'complete community'; (b)
the idea that such a nation-state possesses a civic soul or spirit—a unifying public culture, which can be represented, legitimated, perfected, and protected by a public moral-political
theory.

Many of these same liberal ideas and assumptions have been
accepted by other contemporary sociopolitical theorists who
wish to dispute certain claims of the theorists of contemporary

political liberalism about public morality and policy. In chapter 4 I discuss, briefly, the theory of neonatural law and that of public theology/ethics as presenting alternative accounts of the soul or 'public political culture' of a contemporary liberal democratic nation, such as the United States. These accounts stand in opposition to political liberalism's de-teleologized, secular, and supposedly morally/philosophically neutral account. To consider one such alternative account, the theme of many contributions to a recent collection of papers by American Catholic social thinkers is a confidence that certain aspects of Catholic social thought can supply the "foundation upon which the new and better public philosophy we so urgently need can be constructed,"[1] while preserving intact—indeed, celebrating—the American tradition of religious pluralism.

I shall dispute the existence of such civic souls or public cultures for contemporary Western democracies and, consequently, their use to undergird the project of constructing a public moral-political theory or ethic or theology—i.e., their employment to achieve the illusory stance of nonpartisan neutrality. At the conclusion of chapter 4, I shall outline—again, quite briefly—an alternative picture of what I term the 'politics of imperfection', a pragmatic and prudential attitude toward the political realm that is suitable to the partisan environment of democratic politics. I readily admit that we denizens of postmodern Western liberal democracies perhaps are missing something valuable because our nation-states (or the other, subsidiary forms of polity to which we belong) do not more fully instantiate complete community. The 'politics of perfection' has its attractions; and perhaps it is even true, in some absolute and unconditional sense, that Kenneth Grasso is correct in claiming that we do "urgently need" a "new and better public philosophy." When it comes to praxis, however, what is preferable in an absolute and unconditional sense is often not very pertinent. In view of the religious, moral, and philosophical pluralism that characterizes the democracies of the contemporary West, there is little reason to think that any political theorist can 'stop History' by the construction of a public political theory or public ethic or theology, which all rational, reasonable, and decent citizens *should* be able to endorse in principle as a moral matter. More controversially, I claim that, *at least under the present circumstances*, there is no compelling reason to *want* thus to stop History. In a different world, characterized by considerably more religious, moral, and cultural homogeneity and by mechanisms for a higher level of social and political, as well as economic, control and planning, there is little doubt that a public legitimating political theory (or public ethics or public theology) would be more feasible. In such circumstances it would also perhaps be more desirable. But the absence of an *actual* public theory of this sort (as opposed to various claimants to the title) is not to be remedied by the discovery of some as yet unnoticed theoretical gambit or by more "dialogue" or by heightened "sensitivity" on the part of the citizens of a contemporary Western democracy such as the United States. Rather, the lack of such a theory is a corollary (to all appearances a necessary corollary, although historical appearances can certainly be deceptive) of Modernity and its political manifestations.

Lest this thesis seem to threaten the job security of political philosophers, ethicists, or theologians, I hasten to point out that it in no way undermines the validity of such theoretical activity—including forms of such activity that claim objectivity and a universally obligatory character for their pronouncements. It simply recognizes what I take to be the fact that, in contemporary Western democracies, all such theorizing—at least if it is to proceed beyond the level of ambiguous platitude—will be sectarian or partisan in the following non-pejorative sense of these terms: it will typically make use of principles, attitudes, and methodological assumptions that there is no reason to expect—including no moral reason to expect—that all rational, reasonable, decent, and otherwise mentally and morally nondefective citizens will endorse. Recognition of the partisan and sectarian in contemporary political theory seems to me to be no vice. And the *presence* of the partisan and the sectarian in the contemporary public life of Western democracies, whether a vice or not, is a fact of life that we probably would be well advised to come to terms with in the best way that we can.

Note

1. Kenneth L. Grasso, introduction to *Catholicism, Liberalism, and Communitarianism: The Catholic Intellectual Tradition and the Moral Foun-*

dations of Democracy, ed. K. L. Grasso, G. V. Bradley, and R. P. Hunt (Lanham, Md.: Rowman and Littlefield Publishers, Inc., 1995), 11. The volume does contain some polite but, in my view, perceptive dissent. See in the same volume, e.g., Stanley Hauerwas, "The Importance of Being Catholic: Unsolicited Advice from a Protestant Bystander," 219–34. In my discussion of the neo-natural law tradition I shall, in effect, endorse a comment by Hauerwas: "Natural law underwrote the assumption that Catholic moral theology could be written for anyone irrespective of his/her relation to faith in Jesus of Nazareth. But 'anyone' in America turned out to be the 'individual' of the Enlightenment whose very being depended on the refusal to acknowledge or spell out his/her particular history" (226). In other words (again, those of Hauerwas), "when Catholics came to America they learned that their 'natural law' ethic was community and tradition specific, but it is not yet a lesson they have taken to heart" (222). In the following chapters I shall maintain that the appeal by theorists of political liberalism to notions such as public reason, ideal discourse, rationality/reasonableness as grounding a supposedly nonpartisan and neutral but morally legitimating public political theory indicates that those theorists have not yet taken an analogous lesson to heart.

Acknowledgments

I take pleasure in acknowledging the criticism, advice, and encouragement that I received from many professional colleagues and friends during my work on this book. Among these, I should especially like to mention Professors Richard K. Dagger, Joan L. McGregor, and Jeffrie G. Murphy of Arizona State University, Professor Robert P. George of Princeton University, Professor John P. Hittinger of the United States Air Force Academy, and Professor James Sterba of the University of Notre Dame. I should also like to thank the members of the Arizona State University Moral-Political-Legal (ASUMPL) theory discussion group for helpful and collegial discussion on an earlier draft of chapter 2. Finally, my thanks to Arizona State University and its College of Liberal Arts and Sciences for a sabbatical leave during the 1995–96 academic year, when most of the work on the manuscript was completed.

Chapter 1

Political Liberalism: An Overview

"Political liberalism," suggests Francis Fukuyama, "can be defined simply as a rule of law that recognizes certain individual rights or freedoms from government control."[1] For my present purposes, however, this definition is a bit *too* simple. A comment by John Rawls, the eminent contemporary proponent of political liberalism, although not a definition of political liberalism, gets closer to the heart of the matter: "Given the fact of the reasonable pluralism of democratic culture, the aim of political liberalism is to uncover the conditions of the possibility of a reasonable public basis of justification on fundamental political questions."[2] Political liberalism begins, of course, with the classical liberal tradition alluded to by Fukuyama. That is, it begins with a set of features associated with the political culture inherited by contemporary constitutional democracies, e.g., the idea that political authority derives from some form of consent of citizens, an assumption that some sort of political equality characterizes (or should characterize) the citizens, and an emphasis on some conception of freedom—or some set of liberties—that it is a primary task of political organization to secure and protect. But the defining feature of political liberalism as an influential contemporary movement in political theory is its search for a justification of the fundamentals of liberal polity that does not rely on what Rawls calls a "comprehensive doctrine" or "comprehensive conception of the good"—some richly normative religious, moral, or philosophical conception of human nature, purpose, and destiny. Consequently, political liberalism adopts a stance of neutrality with respect to competing conceptions of the human good or *telos*.

1

From the outset, then, political liberalism sets for itself what
seems to be a formidable intellectual task: justifying a form of
polity and a set of foundational principles associated with that
form of polity without appeal to any determinate account of
what human existence, at the most important level, is all about.

Much of this book will be devoted to arguing that the task
political liberalism has set for itself is not only formidable—
it is forlorn. This task involves a search for what I shall call a
'tertium quid'—some third thing. That third thing is not (a) a
theory justifying democratic political institutions and liberal
sociopolitical principles that is partisan in the sense of appealing to basic principles concerning human life that might
not be acceptable to all rational and decent citizens. Nor is it
(b) the simple acceptance of the historically conditioned
and unsystematic output of more-or-less democratic processes.
Later in this chapter, I shall suggest that there are reasons for
liberal theorists to want to avoid (a), particularly in view of
their common historical conception of liberalism as growing out
of post-Reformation compromise and consensus. There are also
reasons for such theorists to want to avoid (b), which may seem
to be a matter of giving up on the enterprise of the moral justification of sociopolitical institutions and principles altogether. However, a principal thesis of this book, which I shall
attempt to substantiate in this and later chapters, is that the
search for such a tertium quid is ultimately a search for a will-
o'-the-wisp. First, however, I turn to the rather obvious question of why political liberalism has committed itself to such a
task—why, in other words, has it all but guaranteed the failure of its enterprise. For an initial answer to this question we
must turn to two elements of the social and intellectual history of classical modern Europe: the religious pluralism and attendant civil strife in the wake of the Protestant Reformation
and the skeptical challenge at the heart of so much classical
modern philosophical and scientific thought.

The Reformation: Sociopolitical Disaster
or *Felix Culpa*?

John Rawls has particularly emphasized the import of the
former historical moment for political liberalism. The Protestant Reformation of the sixteenth century, he says,

fragmented the religious unity of the Middle Ages and led to religious pluralism, with all its consequences for later centuries. This
in turn fostered pluralisms of other kinds, which were a perma-
nent feature of culture by the end of the eighteenth century. . . .

Thus, the historical origin of political liberalism (and of liberalism more generally) is the Reformation and its aftermath, with the
long controversies over religious toleration in the sixteenth and
seventeenth centuries.[3]

For Rawls, central among—and paradigmatic of—the classical
liberal freedoms is the freedom of thought or conscience that
developed out of what was initially a modus vivendi reluctantly
accepted as a necessary condition of political cooperation in
religiously fragmented northern Europe:

How might a constitutional consensus come about? Suppose that
at a certain time, because of various historical events and contingencies, certain liberal principles of justice are accepted as a mere
modus vivendi, and are incorporated into existing political institutions. This acceptance has come about, let us say, in much the
same way as the acceptance of the principle of toleration came
about as a modus vivendi following the Reformation: at first reluctantly, but nevertheless as providing the only workable alternative to endless and destructive civil strife. Our question, then,
is this: how might it happen that over time the initial acquiescence in a constitution satisfying these liberal principles of justice
develops into a constitutional consensus in which those principles
themselves are affirmed?[4]

Thus, the social fragmentation attendant on the Reformation
that afflicted northern and northwestern Europe looms large in
the historical consciousness of Rawls and, I think, many other
proponents of political liberalism. The Reformation's fragmentation of western Christendom was a Memorable Thing—and
certainly not an unqualified disaster, according to liberal historiography. In fact, all things considered and perhaps a bit
paradoxically, it proved to be a Good Thing. The religious modi
vivendi to which it gave rise are viewed by many liberal theorists as a necessary (?) historical moment along the way to
the principled endorsement of freedom of conscience and the
other fundamental liberties of political liberalism. Most modern writers of "universal histories," which histories generally
picture large-scale historical episodes as moments in "man's

progressive rise to full rationality,"[5] have come from the tradition of liberal Protestantism. It is perhaps then not so peculiar
that what was a rather limited historical episode culturally
and geographically should have been accorded such theoretical significance. Had the Counter Reformation had the success
in northwestern Europe that it enjoyed elsewhere in Europe,
or had the Erastian character of much of eastern Christianity
prevailed in western Europe, the post-Reformation modus vivendi might have remained just that, a temporary, make-shift
accommodation rather than a harbinger of principled political liberalism.

 If there is a value beyond that of contingent and historically and geographically limited expediency in the religious and
other liberties that derived, according to the historiography
typically associated with political liberalism, from post-
Reformation political modi vivendi, then it becomes important
to find some basis of justification of those liberties and the liberal polity in which they have become embedded. That is, justification of some sort becomes significantly more important as
a result of commitment to the stability of the liberal aftermath
of the post-Reformation compromise. Such a commitment is
likely to rest on some principled endorsement of the liberal
compromise. After all, most of those who regard it as only a
regrettably necessary modus vivendi—as, according to Rawls,
most of the parties to the compromise originally did regard it—
would be happier with some alternative political outcome were
it practicable. Consequently, they could not be faulted for lack
of rationality in continuing to search for means to make such
an alternative outcome practicable. Moreover, contemporary political liberals will point out that it would be bizarre to suppose that one could find a basis of justification in one of the
religious traditions that supposedly gave rise to the "endless
and destructive civil strife"[6] in the first place.

 Where else to look? The classical liberal responses seem to
fall into two, not always distinct, categories: (1) an overlapping consensus of comprehensive doctrines, secular or religious,
to whatever degree and in whatever form such consensus could
be found; (2) an appropriate secularized (philosophical or
moral) conception of human nature, purpose, and destiny (that
is, a Rawlsian "comprehensive conception of the good").

Classical Liberalism: Justifying Compromises

The basis of both these approaches to justification is, in contemporary terminology, 'perfectionist'. That is, such a basis of justification makes some claims about the nature, purpose, and destiny of human life and thus is teleological, in a rather broad and inclusive sense of the term. In the words of Will Kymlicka,

> A perfectionist theory includes a particular view, or range of views, about what dispositions and attributes define human perfection, and it views the development of these as our essential interest. Perfectionists demand that resources should be distributed so as to encourage such development. . . . People make mistakes about the good life, and the state has the responsibility to teach its citizens about a virtuous life. It abandons that responsibility to its citizens if it funds, or perhaps even if it tolerates, life-plans that embody misconceived views about human excellence.[7]

The original liberal idea with respect to justification was to formulate a *compromise* perfectionist theory, which would prescind from what was considered inessential (particularly with respect to religious dogma) and include only what were taken to be rationally incontrovertible assumptions concerning human nature, destiny, and purpose. Of course, it is not surprising that exactly what was comprehended by a given liberal compromise tended toward a mixture of (a) what was generally agreed upon within the geographically and temporally local intellectual culture and (b) the philosophical, moral, and religious prepossessions of the particular theorist who was engaged in a program of justification. Here I shall proceed to consider in some detail two rather different historical cases of this classical liberal enterprise, that of John Locke and of Immanuel Kant. A conviction motivating this discussion is that historical considerations pertaining to the roots of liberalism are of considerable use in gaining a clearer conceptual understanding of contemporary political liberalism and gaining insight into its strengths and weaknesses. Indeed, the reader is forewarned that I shall be following this historical conceptual approach throughout the remainder of the book.

That stalwart liberal theorist—the English philosopher John

Locke—presents a noteworthy example of the development of a religious-philosophical theory in order to support an essentially historically contingent religious compromise. To begin with, Locke accepts—as did most of his English contemporaries—an essentially Protestant conception of the privacy and 'inwardness' of the Christian faith: "true and salubrious religion consists in the internal persuasion of mind (*interna animi fide*)."[8] Moreover, men are "all the workmanship of one omnipotent, and infinitely wise maker; all the servants of one sovereign master, sent into the world by his order, and about his business; they are his property, whose workmanship they are, made to last during his, not one another's pleasure."[9] And, says Locke, the "church seems to me to be a free society of men joining together of their own accord, that they may publicly worship God in that manner that they believe shall be acceptable to Deity for the salvation of their souls."[10] With such a set of principles, it is small wonder that Locke remarks that religious toleration is "so consonant with the Gospel and with reason, that it seems monstrous, as it were, that men should be blind in so clear a light."[11]

As Raymond Klibansky notes, Locke's theoretical support of toleration—"legal indulgence allowed to deviations from established orthodoxy"—was "partly a matter of party politics in England."[12] After the partly religiously motivated strife leading up to and following the Civil War earlier in the seventeenth century, there had been a growing movement to extend toleration to various stripes of Protestant nonconformism. At the Restoration, Charles II had promised, in the Declaration of Breda, limited toleration to "tender consciences." And James II, in his two Declarations of Indulgence, hoped to win nonconformist support for what was, in intent, a policy for procuring toleration for Roman Catholics. After the "Glorious Revolution" had bolstered Whig fortunes—and in 1689 four years after Locke's composition of the *Epistola de Tolerantia*—a Toleration Act limited to Protestant nonconformism (and excluding Catholics, Unitarians, Jews, and atheists) passed both houses of Parliament and was signed by William and Mary.

Locke's exclusions, in his *de Tolerantia*, of Roman Catholics and atheists[13] from the umbrella of toleration also reflected a Protestant consensus: The civil order is threatened by the Catholic claim that the Church has the authority to absolve subjects of allegiance to their sovereign by the act of excommunication (as was done by Pius V with respect to Elizabeth I in the bull *Regnans in excelsis* of 1570). Furthermore, Protestants who doubted that Catholics could be trusted as participants in a civil policy of religious toleration, often pointed to an extreme version of the Catholic doctrine of 'mental reservation' interpreted as entailing that "no faith need be kept with heretics."[14]

In his claim that "those who deny that Deity exists are in no manner to be tolerated" (because "neither trust nor contract nor oath, which are the bonds of human society, can be anything stable or sacred to the atheist"[15]), Locke is simply expressing a widely accepted view of the period. But in his *Essay concerning Human Understanding*, he supports this exclusion with theory. In support of his latitudinarian convictions about a rational and ethical 'fundamental core' of Christianity, he proposes that the requirements of morality can, in principle, be exhibited as a deductive system of relations among ideas:

> The *Idea* of a supreme Being, infinite in Power, Goodness, and Wisdom, whose Workmanship we are, and on whom we depend; and the *Idea* of our selves, as understanding, rational Beings, being such as are clear in us, would, I suppose, if duly considered, and pursued, afford such Foundations of our Duty and Rules of Action as might place *Morality amongst the Sciences capable of Demonstration*: wherein I doubt not, but from self-evident Propositions, by necessary Consequences, as incontestible as those in Mathematicks, the measures of right and wrong might be made out, to any one that will apply himself with the same Indifferency and Attention to the one, as he does to the other of these Sciences.[16]

Thus Locke is led, famously, to conclude that *"Morality is the proper Science, and Business of Mankind in general; (who are both concerned, and fitted to search out their Summum Bonum,) as several Arts, conversant about several parts of Nature, are the Lot and private Talent of particular Men"* (chap. 12, 646). While the *content* of our moral and essential religious obligations may be a matter of demonstration, the motivation for fulfilling such obligations is another matter. Locke's account of the 'springs of action' or motivation for human behavior is entirely hedonistic: *"That which is properly good or bad, is nothing but barely Pleasure or Pain"* (bk. 2, chap. 21, 274).

The fact that, on Locke's reconsidered view, what "deter-

mines the will" or moves us to action is our "present uneasi-
ness," rather than our present conception of our overall "greatest good," largely explains moral error—mistaken choices about
what is conducive to our greatest good. With respect to this
mortal life, however, human beings notoriously differ with respect to what gives them pleasure (identified with their *bonum*): "the Mind has a different relish, as well as the Palate; and
you will as fruitlessly endeavor to delight all Men with Riches
or Glory, (which yet some Men place their Happiness in,) as
you would to satisfy all Men's Hunger with Cheese or Lobsters"
(269). Consequently, says Locke, "if there be no Prospect beyond the Grave, the inference is certainly right, *Let us eat and
drink,* let us enjoy what we delight in, *for to morrow we shall
die*" (270).

It is our belief in the existence of God, with the attendant threat of incommensurable pain and promise of incommensurable pleasure, that supplies motivation to conform
with the demonstrable obligations of reason (and 'reasonable Christianity'):

> Change but a Man's view of these things; let him see, that Virtue
> and Religion are necessary to his Happiness; let him look into the
> future State of Bliss or Misery, and see there God, the righteous
> Judge, ready to *render to every Man according to his Deeds*. . . . To
> him, I say, who hath a prospect of the different State of perfect
> Happiness or Misery, that attends all Men after this Life, depend-
> ing on their Behaviour here, the measures of Good and Evil, that
> govern his choice, are mightily changed. For since nothing of Plea-
> sure or Pain in this Life, can bear any proportion to the endless
> Happiness, or exquisite Misery of an immortal Soul hereafter,
> Actions in his Power will have their preference . . . as they serve
> to secure that perfect durable Happiness hereafter (273-74).

The extreme hedonism underlying Locke's conception of moral
motivation certainly succeeds in justifying or legitimating his
exclusion of atheists from the *Epistola de Tolerantia*'s umbrella
of toleration.

But does it *persuasively* justify it—even from the perspective of Locke's contemporaries? Yes—for those who accept his
psychological hedonism, who endorse his affirmation of the existence of a God able and willing to grant "endless happiness
or exquisite misery". But most of these premises were contro-

versial in Locke's time and before, as they are in our own. My
point in discussing Locke in some detail at this relatively early
juncture is to illustrate something that seems to me misguided
about the attempt to ground or justify, theoretically, the contingent outcome of sociopolitical compromise and the modi
vivendi to which it gives rise. Typically, the 'theoretical infra-
structure' proves to be more controversial than the collection
of doctrines or practices comprehended in the compromise that
the theory is supposed to secure and stabilize. It is a matter of
justifying or stabilizing the *controversiale per controversialius.*

When we meditate on this situation a bit, it does not seem
surprising. We are accustomed to the idea that a theory, say, in
the natural sciences, is 'underdetermined' by a given, finite set
of phenomena that it is to explain. That such a theory has implications that transcend the given data set on the basis of
which it was developed is generally regarded as a good and
useful thing. Such additional implications may provide the basis
on which the theory may be tested against alternative theories
that also adequately explain the original data set. But the relationship between a sociopolitical compromise or modus
vivendi ("data set") and a theory that is supposed to justify,
ground, secure, or stabilize such a compromise is quite different. It is obvious that the need for the compromise generally
arises because of conflicting world views or, in Rawlsese, "comprehensive doctrines." The compromise itself represents limited areas where agreement can be reached—usually by the
political give-and-take of relenting on the inessential and pa-
pering over, as much as possible, substantive disagreement
about the basis and implications of what is being agreed to.
Usually, an attempt at theoretical justification of the product of
compromise is, in effect, to ask the parties to the compromise
to agree to more—and often to agree on more by way of *fundamental* matters—than is comprehended by the compromise itself. Obviously, it is seldom an effective strategy for securing
or stabilizing an agreement to which the parties have been led
to assent for a variety of diverse reasons to add more issues of
potential or actual disagreement or to ask people to compromise on more rather than less. In other words, when a theory
is supposed to justify or legitimate the result of concrete political compromise, the fact that the theory is more coherent or
systematic or 'deeper' than what it is intended to justify, the

fact that it has implications that transcend that 'data set', seems generally not to be an advantage in terms of its achieving the public justification that is its purpose.

Insofar as this problem was recognized by classical liberals, it did not much deter them from constructing justifying or grounding theories in support of various features of liberal modi vivendi. No doubt this was so largely because such classical liberals were much more inclined to view their theory construction as a search for truth than as means for stabilizing or entrenching, in the sociopolitical sphere, the liberal modi vivendi. With the Enlightenment came the assumption that a secularized justifying theory, appealing only to rationally incontrovertible premises, would likely be the best means for getting at the "underlying truth of liberal modi vivendi." The justifying theory would also thus be built on neutral ground, independent of personal religious persuasion and other nonrational idiosyncrasies, and have the potential of wide acceptance—at least in the long run. We have here, then, the Enlightenment hope that "man's progressive rise to full rationality," in the words of Fukuyama, would issue in "self-conscious awareness of how that rationality expresses itself in liberal self-government."[17]

The preeminent illustration of an attempt to justify liberal polity by deriving it from human rationality is surely provided by Immanuel Kant. *Practical* rationality, the employment of reason as a means for attaining certain ends, was considered, in a classical tradition extending back at least to Aristotle, to involve a collaboration with desire or appetite. As Aristotle puts it in the *Nicomachean Ethics*,

> What affirmation and denial are in thinking, pursuit and avoidance are in desire. So that, since moral virtue is a character state concerned with choice, and choice is deliberative desire, it is therefore necessary that the reason be true and the desire correct if the choice is to be good, and that desire do what reason says. This sort of thinking and truth is practical. The good and the bad state of theoretical thinking—not of practical nor productive—consists in truth and falsity, respectively (for this is the function of everything having the capacity of thought). But the good state of that which is practical and has the capacity of thought is truth in agreement with desire that is right.[18]

According to this classical conception of practical reason, the desire that practical reason involves need not (but may) be conceived in hedonistic or egoistic terms. Indeed, in one version of the theory of natural law, the "desire" or *appetitus naturalis* to achieve some objective "human good" or *telos* supplies the foundation of morality. This *telos* can be complex and hierarchical, as for St. Thomas Aquinas, or the simple and relatively straightforward avoidance of death and harm, as for Hobbes. But it has normative import, which is nicely characterized by Alasdair MacIntyre:

> Within the teleological scheme there is fundamental contrast between man-as-he-happens-to-be and man-as-he-could-be-if-he-realised-his-essential-nature. Ethics is the science which is to enable men to understand how they make the transition from the former to the latter. Ethics therefore on this view presupposes some account of potentiality and act, some account of the essence of man as a rational animal and above all some account of the human *telos*. The precepts which enjoin the various virtues and prohibit the various vices which are their counterparts instruct us how to move from potentiality to act, how to realise our true nature and to reach our true end. To defy them will be to be frustrated and incomplete, to fail to achieve that good of rational happiness which it is peculiarly ours as a species to pursue.[19]

MacIntyre maintains that the combined effect of Protestantism, Jansenist Catholicism, and Enlightenment secularism (particularly in its rejection of Aristotelian scholastic philosophy and science) was "to eliminate any notion of man-as-he-could-be-if-he-realised-his-*telos*" and, thus, radically to transform the idea of morality:

> There is on the one hand a certain content for morality: a set of injunctions deprived of the teleological context. There is on the other hand a certain view of untutored-human-nature-as-it-is. Since the moral injunctions were originally at home in a scheme in which their purpose was to correct, improve and educate that human nature, they are clearly not going to be such that they could be deduced from true statements about human nature or justified in some other way by appealing to its characteristics. The injunctions of morality, thus understood, are likely to be ones that human nature, thus understood, has strong tendencies to disobey (52-53).

MacIntyre regards Kant as an ambivalent figure with respect to this transformation. On the one hand, Kant "looks for a foundation of morality in the universalizable prescriptions of reason"; but, on the other hand, he maintains rigorous "strictures against founding morality on human nature" (53). The ambivalence is explained, of course, by Kant's conception of *pure*, as opposed to empirically conditioned or determined, practical reason. Pure practical reason supplies, as it were, its own *telos*, rather than obtaining its end or ends as "givens", external to reason in a narrow sense. It is clear that Kant thinks that any such externally given end would be an empirical *telos* of MacIntyre's untutored-human-nature-as-it-happens-to-be; the possibility of a given end, external to reason in the narrow sense, exemplifying human-nature-as-it-could-be-if-it-realised-its-*telos* has simply disappeared. The remaining empirical *telē* of untutored-human-nature-as-it-happens-to-be cannot ground the universality that Kant ascribes to moral imperatives, as he makes clear in the *Critique of Practical Reason*:

> Is therefore astonishing how intelligent men have thought of proclaiming as a universal practical law the desire for happiness, and therewith to make this desire the determining ground of the will merely because this desire is universal. Though elsewhere natural laws make everything harmonious, if one here attributed the universality of law to this maxim, there would be extreme opposite of harmony, the most arrant conflict, and the complete annihilation of the maxim itself and its purpose. For the wills of all do not have one and the same object, but each person has his own (his own welfare), which, to be sure, can accidentally agree with the purposes of others who are pursuing their own, though this agreement is far from sufficing for a law because the occasional exceptions which one is permitted to make are endless and cannot be definitely comprehended in a universal rule.[20]

In order for pure reason to be practical, then, "it must be able to determine the will by the mere form of the practical rule without presupposing any feeling or consequently any idea of the pleasant or the unpleasant as the matter of the faculty of desire and as the empirical conditions of its principles" (23 [vol. 6, 24]). Rational morality must be self-contained or autonomous: the very universalizability of a principle, the declaration of it "by reason to be a law for all rational beings insofar as they have a will, i.e., a faculty of determining their causality through the conception of a rule" (32 [32]), becomes the sole legitimate source of moral motivation:

> The *autonomy* of the will is the sole principle of all moral laws and of the duties conforming to them. . . .
> The sole principle of morality consists in independence from all material of the law (i. e., a desired object) and in the accompanying determination of choice by the mere form of giving universal law which a maxim must be capable of having. . . . Therefore, the moral law expresses nothing else than the autonomy of the pure practical reason, i.e., freedom (33-34 [34]).

However, Kant holds that the moral subject in his 'phenomenal existence', considered as a part of the spatiotemporal nexus of causal relations, is always subject to natural necessity: that is, his or her choices are always—from the phenomenal, scientific perspective—dependent on factors external to reason and, thus, are heteronomously determined. To find the autonomy or freedom that is a necessary condition of morality, as Kant has reconceptualized it, he must look to the noumenal realm:

> But the same subject, which, on the other hand, is conscious of his own existence as a thing-in-itself, also views his existence so far as it does not stand under temporal conditions, and to himself as determinable only by laws which he gives to himself through reason. In this existence nothing is antecedent to the determination of his will; every action . . . is seen in the consciousness of his intelligible existence as only a consequence, not as a determining ground of his causality as a noumenon. From this point of view, a rational being can rightly say of any unlawful action which he has done that he could have left it undone, even if as an appearance it was sufficiently determined in the past and thus far was inescapably necessary (101 [97-98]).

With respect to the phenomenal realm, the realm of possible experience with which science (and what we think of as everyday life) is concerned, Kant is a determinist. But with respect to the demands of morality he is a rigorous incompatibilist. For an action to be virtuously performed, it must be performed simply because it is virtuous, a duty that is universalizable and thus prescribed for every rational creature; and this requirement he interprets as requiring a radical autonomy of choice—the capacity to have done otherwise. Consequently, he concludes that such autonomy belongs to the noumenal rather than the empirical or phenomenal self. Indeed, we have knowledge of this autonomy only because of a 'transcendental argument', the consequence of the facts that (a) we are aware within ourselves of the demands of morality and (b) we recognize that autonomy/freedom is a necessary condition of moral action.

This transcendental autonomy equally possessed by all persons is, not surprisingly, put to political use by Kant. To quote John Ladd, "the basis of man's right to liberty is the fact that he is an autonomous moral being, that is a sovereign lawmaker, as well as subject to the law (the moral law)."[21] Thus, for Kant (as for Rousseau) justice becomes "the aggregate of those conditions under which the will of one person can be conjoined with the will of another in accordance with a universal law of freedom."[22] The primary purpose of political organization is to provide the context for citizens to fulfill their nature as autonomous moral agents, not to provide for their common good or happiness (conceived again as the empirical desiderata of untutored-human-nature-as-it-happens-to-be, not the ideal, normative desiderata of human-nature-as-it-could-be-if-it-realised-its-*telos*):

> In regard to the first issue (happiness), no universally valid principles can be laid down as laws. For both the temporal circumstances and the deeply conflicting and thus continually changing illusions in which each person places happiness (though no one can prescribe for another where he should place it) make all fixed principles impossible, and happiness is in itself unfit as principle underlying legislation. The proposition *salus publica suprema civitatis lex est* [the public welfare is the supreme law of the state] remains undiminished in value and esteem; but the [aspect of the] public's well being to receive *first* consideration is precisely that legal contract securing everyone's freedom through laws, that contract whereby each person remains at liberty to seek his happiness in any way he thinks best so long as he does not violate that universal freedom under the law and, consequently, the rights of other fellow subjects.[23]

The "supreme task nature has set for the human species," says Kant, is the attainment of a "society in which one will find the highest possible degree of *freedom under external laws* combined with irresistible power; . . . for only by solving and completing [this task] can nature fulfill her other objectives with our species."[24] Here Kant's Enlightenment brand of determinism manifests itself. Since constitutions and political actions belong to the phenomenal, empirical realm, they must be governed by universal natural laws:

> Whatever concept one may form of *freedom of the will* in a metaphysical context, its *appearances*, human actions, like all other natural events are certainly determined in conformity with universal natural laws. History—which concerns itself with providing a narrative of these appearances, regardless of how deeply hidden their causes may be—allows us to hope that if we examine *the play of the human will's freedom in the large*, we can discover its course to conform to rules as well as to hope that what strikes us as complicated and unpredictable in the single individual may in the history of the entire species be discovered to be the steady progress and slow development of its original capacities.[25]

Deterministic historical processes, then, eventually yield forms of polity that are liberal and "republican." Kant's "First Definitive Article of Perpetual Peace" is that the

> civil constitution of every nation should be republican. . . . For, first, it accords with the principles of the *freedom* of the members of a society (as men), second, it accords with the principle of the *dependence* of everyone on a single, common [source of] legislation (as subjects), and third, it accords with the law of the equality of them all (as citizens).[26]

In the light of the universal history sketched in "Idea for a Universal History," Kant's endorsement of liberal republicanism is not merely normative or, in Marx' pejorative terminology, "utopian": liberal republicanism is the eventual outcome of the laws of nature as they operate on human social interactions.

As in the case of Locke, Kant begins with ideas that were, by his time, becoming increasingly common. Although most of these ideas had ancient pedigrees, they were revived in Enlightenment thought. We find in Kant (1) the notion (diametrically opposed to that of Locke) that the practice of virtue should be its own goal and reward, (2) an essentially moralizing conception of religion, which locates the core of Christian theism in rational morality, (3) the conviction that the 'mature' fulfillment of human nature lies in the rational autonomy of the individual person's *Wille* (rational will), (4) a conception of political authority as devolving from the will of the individual citizen and, consequently, (5) a generally sympathetic attitude toward republicanism (despite the "excesses" of the French).

These elements of the developing liberal consensus find grounding and justification in Kant's elaborate metaphysical scheme, which I have just sketched. That metaphysical grounding is not only elaborate but heavy-duty, factory-strength; as in the case of Locke, Kant's theory proved more controversial than the consensus that it was supposed to justify. Of course, this fact does not signify that there is something wrong if the principal purpose of a justifying theory is to get at the "deeper truth" of which a liberal compromise or modus vivendi is believed to be a manifestation. There is little doubt that this was the conviction of Kant, as well as of most other classical liberal theorists. But a crucial assumption of contemporary *political* liberalism is that the function of a justifying or grounding theory is principally political: that is, it is supposed to be maximally acceptable to citizens within modern constitutional democracies and, thus, is supposed to fulfill the political function of underwriting and stabilizing the liberal compromise. From such a perspective, "spooky" Kantian metaphysics (like Locke's retributive theism) becomes a liability of the sort noted by Charles Larmore:

> Tying liberalism so closely to a controversial personal ideal (whatever its validity) [i.e., Kant's metaphysical notion of personal autonomy] has made liberalism itself needlessly vulnerable. Anti-liberals could now attack the ideal of political neutrality by criticizing the ideal of personal autonomy.[27]

In Kantian metaphysics we apparently have come a long way from the concrete historical experience—the Reformation fragmentation of western Christendom—that many contemporary political liberals see as originally giving rise to the modern liberal modi vivendi. But in the reservations of theorists of political liberalism concerning classical perfectionist attempts by Kant (and others) to justify such liberal compromises, we see the second element—alluded to at the beginning of this chapter—that figures prominently in the historical consciousness associated with contemporary political liberalism: skepticism.

The Skeptical Beast: *Noire ou Belle?*

Contemporary theorists of liberalism have been much less ready to acknowledge the historical or conceptual role of skepticism in the development of political liberalism than the role of post-Reformation religious modi vivendi. Particularly since the 1950s historians of modern philosophy, led by the dean of historians of skepticism, Richard Popkin, have succeeded in establishing the centrality of skeptical concerns in the development of modern thought, both philosophical and scientific. So it should not be surprising to find skepticism playing a key role in the development of sociopolitical thought. However, neither folk psychology nor history presents a neat, clear, and simple picture of the rôle of skepticism in the etiology of liberal neutrality. Folk psychology or common sense is apparently ambiguous, as is often the case. On the one hand, common sense tells us (a) that the adoption of a stance of neutrality or compromise on an issue is more attractive the less the issue in question matters to us or the less important we deem it to be and (b) that *one* reason that we may be inclined to regard an issue as unimportant is skepticism as to whether there is a truth or fact of the matter to be discovered with respect to the issue—or whether human beings have the capacity, in principle, of discerning such a truth if there is one. Thus, for example, I *may* be inclined to adopt a laissez-faire attitude toward abortion if I am skeptical about whether there is any fact of the matter, beyond conventional stipulation, about whether a fetus is a person. On the other hand, it is a commonplace of folk psychology that skeptical doubts about a matter can precipitate or confirm in the doubter rigidly dogmatic attitudes with respect to the matter in question. Perhaps the principal moral here, to which I shall return, is that there is considerable difference, and certainly no invariant logical relation, between not caring about a proposition, theory, or doctrine—or judging it to be unimportant—and being skeptical or uncertain about the epistemological basis of such a proposition, theory, or doctrine.

   With respect to the history of liberal toleration and skepticism, the record is also ambiguous. Skepticism, as a revived
intellectual tradition from Greek antiquity, was employed in
Reformation religious controversies. In behalf of what was a
misguided attempt to promote irenicism, Erasmus in his dispute of 1524-25 with Luther concerning the freedom of the will
remarks that "so far am I from delighting in 'assertions' that I
would readily take refuge in the opinion of the Skeptics, wherever this is allowed by the inviolable authority of Holy Scrip-
tures and by the decrees of the Church."[28] Perhaps somewhat
uncharitably, if not implausibly, Luther interprets Erasmus's
skeptical irenicism as being grounded in unbelief:

> In short, what you say here seems to mean that it does not matter
> to you what anyone believes anywhere, so long as the peace of
> the world is undisturbed, and that in case of danger to life, repu-
> tation, property, and goodwill, it is permissible to act like the fel-
> low who said, 'Say they yea, yea say I, say they nay, nay say I,'
> and to regard Christian dogmas as no better than philosophical
> and human opinions, about which it is quite stupid to wrangle,
> contend, assert, ... So, with a view to ending our conflicts, you
> come forward as a mediator, calling a halt to both sides, and try-
> ing to persuade us that we are flourishing our swords about things
> that are stupid and useless.[29]

Some two and one-half centuries later Voltaire, in the article
"Tolerance" of his *Philosophical Dictionary*, is more explicit than
Erasmus in arguing for religious toleration on skeptical grounds:

> Every sect, as we know, is a certificate of error; there are no
> sects of geometers, algebraists, and arithmeticians because all the
> propositions of geometry, algebra, and arithmetic are true. In all
> other sciences, men may make mistakes. What Thomist or Scotist
> theologian would dare to say seriously that he is sure of his
> facts? . . . But it is even clearer that we should all mutually toler-
> ate each other, because we are weak, inconsistent, a prey to change
> and error. Should a reed bowed into the mud by the wind say to
> the neighboring reed, bowed in the opposite direction: "Creep in
> my fashion, wretch, or I'll send in a request to have you uprooted
> and burned"?[30]

   Skepticism, however, was also commonly yoked to fideism
in post-Reformation polemics. That is, skeptical arguments un-

dermine the insalubrious effects of intellectual presumption and thus serve as a propaedeutic for the gift of faith. In the hands of such figures as Michel de Montaigne, Pierre Charron, and François Varon, the pairing of skepticism and fideism grounded a powerful Counter-Reformation polemic on behalf of doctrinal orthodoxy and conservatism. In a famous passage from his "Apologie de Raimond Sebond," Montaigne writes of Pyrrhonian skepticism that

> [t]here is nothing in man's invention that has so much verisimilitude and usefulness. It presents man naked and empty, acknowledging his natural weakness, fit to receive from above some outside power; stripped of human knowledge, and so the more apt to lodge divine knowledge in himself, annihilating his judgment to make more room for faith; neither disbelieving nor setting up any doctrine against the common observances; humble, obedient, teachable, zealous; a sworn enemy of heresy, and consequently free from the vain and irreligious opinions introduced by the false sects.[31]

Of course, the Protestants eventually caught on. Pierre Bayle showed that fideism could be combined, after a fashion, with Calvinism as well as with Catholicism.

As an historical matter, then, skepticism has been invoked to support an attitude of religious toleration; and it could just as well be invoked more generally to support a policy of political laissez-faire neutrality with respect to competing conceptions of the good or *telos* of human beings. But "just as well invoked" does not here imply "well invoked." It will be noted that, in the quotation from Voltaire's *Dictionary,* he does not explain *why* the alleged fact that "we are weak, inconsistent, a prey to change and error" implies that we should tolerate one another. As a logical-conceptual matter, there seems to be good reason to agree with Avrum Stroll that the "skeptical attitude" "provides no ground for supporting intolerance and it provides no ground for supporting tolerance. It is neutral with respect to both of these principles."[32] The same conclusion holds, in my judgment, for the relation between skepticism and a principle of toleration or neutrality with respect to competing conceptions of the human good or *telos.*

Nonetheless, contemporary political liberalism has been accused—typically by communitarian anti-liberals—of relying, at least implicitly, on skepticism to justify its stance of neutrality with respect to conceptions of the good. The typical reaction to this accusation on the part of political liberals has been one of indignant denial. Ronald Dworkin, for example, retorts that "[l]iberalism cannot be based on skepticism. Its constitutive morality provides that human beings must be treated as equals by their government, not because there is no right or wrong in political morality, but because that is what is right."[33] In his later *Law's Empire*, he maintains that few liberals (except Thomas Hobbes, if he counts as a liberal) have "adopted any form of skepticism about the possibility that one way of leading one's life can be better or more valuable than another." One common communitarian critique of liberalism, he continues,

> confuses that form of skepticism, which most liberals reject, with the entirely different principle they accept, that claims about the relative value of personal goals do not provide competent justifications for regulative political decisions. . . . this picture of liberalism confuses *that* principle, about the neutrality of government towards conceptions of the good, with an alleged neutrality about principles of justice, which of course liberalism, because it is a theory of justice, must reject.[34]

Similarly, Will Kymlicka sees the neutrality or toleration of various conceptions of the human good as justified, primarily, because it "provides the best conditions under which people can make informed and rational judgements about the value of different pursuits."[35] The value of the liberal freedoms, then, rests on the assumption that we can be right or wrong, make better or worse decisions about what constitutes a worthwhile human life: "[s]ome projects *are* more worthy than others, and liberty is needed precisely to find out what is valuable in life— to question, re-examine, and revise our beliefs about value."[36]

Among contemporary theorists of political liberalism, Rawls perhaps comes the closest to invoking skepticism regarding conceptions of the good as a reason for adopting a principle of political neutrality or toleration. His phrase "burdens of judgment" connotes all the *reasonable* considerations that make agreement with respect to conceptions of the human *telos* or good difficult or impossible to achieve in the modern world. There certainly are *unreasonable* grounds of disagreement as well: "prejudice and bias, self- and group interest, blindness, and willfulness."[37] But these do not merit the political and moral accommodation that reasonable grounds of disagreement do. It is generally true, Rawls claims, that

> our individual and associative points of view, intellectual affinities, and affective attachments, are too diverse, especially in a free society, to enable those doctrines to serve as the basis of a lasting and reasoned political agreement. Different conceptions of the world can reasonably be elaborated from different standpoints and diversity arises in part from our distinct perspectives (58).

This fact, Rawls concludes, is "of first significance for a democratic idea of toleration" (58). Nonetheless, he is adamant in denying that skepticism lies at the heart of this inference. To begin with, he appeals to a rather narrow conception of skepticism: an epistemological argument, or group of arguments, that "offer[s] a philosophical analysis of the conditions of knowledge" and proceeds to conclude that we cannot have knowledge of some of those, assumed "objects because one or more of the necessary conditions of knowledge can never be satisfied" (63). His own account of "burdens of judgment," in contradistinction to skeptical considerations, is essentially empirical and practical in import: "It simply lists some of the circumstances that make political agreement in judgment, especially in judgments about comprehensive doctrines, far more difficult. This difficulty is borne out by historical experience, by centuries of conflict about religious, philosophical, and moral beliefs" (63). Moreover, the implications of the burdens of judgment apply only to the political realm, to the life of the person as *citoyen* (citizen, or member of the political community), not to the private and associational realms, to the life of the person as *bourgeois* or *homme* (member of civil society):

> Political liberalism does not question that many political and moral judgments of certain specified kinds are correct and it views many of them as reasonable. Nor does it question the possible truth of affirmations of faith. Above all, it does not argue that we should be hesitant and uncertain, much less skeptical, about our own beliefs. Rather, we are to recognize the practical impossibility of reaching reasonable and workable political agreement in judgment on the truth of comprehensive doctrines, especially an agreement

that might serve the political purpose, say, of achieving peace and
concord in a society characterized by religious and philosophical
differences (63).

It must be admitted that many of the charges of skepticism
that have been leveled against the liberal tradition of political
theory are not well founded. Liberalism, including contemporary political liberalism, has its own set of deeply seated dog-
mas (with respect to "the right," anyway, if not always, officially, with respect to "the good") just as more traditional
religious and moral views do. On the other hand, there does
seem to be *some*, perhaps deep and not altogether pellucid,
connection between liberalism and epistemological considerations that might reasonably be labeled "skeptical." I shall suggest that there are two loci within the tradition of liberal
political theory where the term "skeptical" might plausibly be
invoked.

The first locus is MacIntyre's notion of human-nature-as-it-
could-be-if-it-realised-its-*telos*. The liberal tradition, including
contemporary political liberalism, is characterized by skepticism
concerning and often repudiation of what I shall call the sociopolitical validity of the concept that such an objective *telos*,
endemic to the species, can serve as a basis for making decisions in conformity with distributive justice. Some contemporary theorists will respond that political liberalism simply
denies a *political* role to such a notion; the fact that political
liberalism does not question or deny the 'truth' of such a conception is demonstrated by the fact that such a *telos* is still per-
mitted as a legitimate constituent of the individual citizen's
personal comprehensive doctrine or conception of the good. The
response to this initial retort is that a good part of such a
notion's normative force is directed toward the social realm
(including the political part of the social realm). To deny or to
circumscribe the political implications of such a concept—
as, for example, the common doctrine of political liberalism does concerning the political priority of the right to the
good—is, in effect, to adopt a stance toward the concept that
could plausibly be described as one either of repudiation or of
skeptical suspense of judgment. The political liberal, in fact,
is objecting to at least some of the sociopolitical claims implicit in the conception of such a human *telos*, often because

there are, in his or her judgment, plenty of reasonable competing conceptions.

Some contemporary political liberals will then proceed to claim that their resistance to the political claims of such a conception is merely pragmatic: the empirical fact of a multiplicity of mutually incompatible notions of this sort current in society means that any attempt to instantiate, politically, one of them would be the source of insupportable civil strife or at least would necessitate, in Rawls's words, the "oppressive use of state power."[38] I do not doubt the sincerity of the conviction of political liberals that the stance of political neutrality with respect to conceptions of the good is the most effective means of achieving and preserving political stability, in a purely descriptive sense of that term. I do doubt, however, that political liberals typically advocate this stance of neutrality *exclusively* on grounds of political expediency, as opposed to principle. For one thing, most liberals seem to be generally well disposed toward the pluralism with respect to conceptions of the good that makes the stance of neutrality politically expedient or necessary in the first place; and they are often willing to adopt social measures, including political ones, to further and preserve that pluralism.

In the case of Rawls, as I shall argue in chapter 3, his very notion of "stability" is a morally normative one. In his view, it simply would be *unfair*, apart from any issues of political workability, to privilege politically a particular conception of the human good or *telos*. Such a moral judgment, based on the equal *reasonableness* of many competing comprehensive doctrines, certainly seems to involve an epistemic attitude that, despite Rawls's protestations, might reasonably termed "skeptical." Although we do not have sufficient reason to proscribe various traditional conceptions of the human *telos* (and various other individual conceptions citizens may form of their individual goods), we also do not have sufficient reason to instantiate or prescribe politically any of these 'reasonable' conceptions—particularly because our doing so would somehow unfairly infringe on the activity of individual citizens, each in forming (rationally, we may hope) his *own* conception of his good and his own life-plan attendant on that conception.

Roberto Mangobeira Unger has argued that the emergence of liberal political theory in modern thought was coincident with the development of a principle of the radical independence of the faculties of understanding and desire. According to this principle, which he calls the "principle of reason and desire," "[t]he mind machine, by itself, wants nothing; desire, unaided by understanding, can see nothing."[39] He regards this principle as rendering the traditional conception of practical reason, as well as MacIntyre's notion of human-nature-as-it-could-be-if-it-realised-its-*telos*, epistemologically suspect. As a result, he says, these 'preliberal' components of moral and political theory have become "alien to our ways of thinking":

> The unfamiliar spirit that animates this preliberal denial of the principle of reason and desire is the conception that what ought to be and what is are not wholly different. In this conception, the ideal does not stand above the world, but is part of it. Values are facts because they have a mode of existence outside the minds of individuals who acknowledge them. And facts themselves, correctly understood, are in a sense already what they ought to become. More concisely put, the intelligible essence of each thing in the world is its ideal. So, for example, according to this view, there is a universally valid ideal of perfected human life. We call this ideal humanity because it distinguishes man from all other kinds of beings. It is his intelligible essence.[40]

I believe that Unger is correct: Skepticism concerning, or outright repudiation of, such a framework for integrating fact and value, a framework that would be applicable to the sociopolitical as well as private realm, is fundamental to the tradition of liberal political thought, including contemporary political liberalism. This, then, is the first locus of skepticism in liberal political theory to which I alluded above. The second locus is found nearby.

In its etymology, the Greek adjective "*skeptikos*" connotes one who looks into, examines, considers, or reflects—not necessarily one who doubts, denies, or scoffs. If, as I and others have suggested, liberal sociopolitical theory repudiates the idea of human-nature-as-it-could-be-if-it-realised-its-*telos* as a normative fact that is regulative of the sociopolitical order and individual lives, then what is left to it for a conception of the human good or *telos*? One could, of course, give up on the idea altogether. In a sense, this is what is done within two, "radical" philosophical traditions. A certain radical version of existentialism has done so: we are, individually, entirely what we make of ourselves by our free but ultimately arbitrary, arational acts of will. At the other extreme, there is a radical biological and/or social determinism: Our individual good is simply that combination of desires, aversions, and preferences that we are determined, individually, to have by our genetic constitution as we are acted upon by the particular social circumstances into which we have been born. In the case of radical existentialism, the notion of a human *telos* has been 'denatured' by having been deprived of any determinate content. In the case of biological-social determinism, it has been denatured by having been deprived of its normative aspect; my individual, customized conception of the good is thrust upon me, willy-nilly, from without, and that I act in conformity to it is simply an empirical fact, apparently without any moral dimension or import. Although, political liberals have generally avoided both these extremes, frequently they have been attracted to a personalized conception of the human good, something that we reflect on, examine, consider, and look into, something that we *may* reconsider, come to doubt, or change our mind about, in the manner of a *skeptikos*—in the original etymological sense of the term.

This conception of the good as something personal, which one adopts, latches onto, or otherwise appropriates, is common to much contemporary liberal thought. For Dworkin, issues concerning the human good, as distinguished from "principles of justice," become "claims about the relative value of personal goals."[41] Kymlicka writes of making "informed and rational judgements about the value of different pursuits."[42] According to Rawls, if we are reasonable, a consequence will be that "[w]e recognize that our own doctrine [of the good] has, and can have, for people generally, no special claims on them beyond their own view of its merits,"[43] which view is formed by a process that involves "singling out which values to count as especially significant and [determining] how to balance them when they conflict."[44] And, in Larmore's estimation,

[i]n modern times we have come to recognize a multiplicity of ways in which a fulfilled life can be lived, without any percepti-

ble hierarchy among them. And we have also been forced to acknowledge that even where we do believe that we have discerned
the superiority of some ways of life to others, reasonable people
may often not share our view. Pluralism and reasonable disagreement have become for modern thought ineliminable features of
the idea of the good life.[45]

What has occurred, in the development of modern liberalism, is a loosening of the bond between individual person or citizen and the old, quasi-factual but normative notion
of human-nature-as-it-could-be-if-it-realised-its-*telos*. Insofar as
skepticism concerning this latter notion has been involved in
the process, liberalism has deemed it to be not at all a *bête noire*
but a bright and lovely emancipator of the individual. Essentially this viewpoint is expressed, in a variety of ways and
within a variety of philosophical contexts, by many contemporary theorists of liberalism. Kymlicka asserts that "our ends
are neither arbitrary nor fixed"—e.g.,"fixed" by a normative-
factual human *telos*. Thus, in one of his favorite phrases, "lives
have to be led from the inside," and this fundamental fact
grounds liberalism's commitment to individual autonomy or
freedom and its toleration of differing conceptions of the good.[46]
Larmore associates especially with Kant the conviction that
"our highest personal ideal ought to incorporate a certain distance or detachment toward conceptions of the good life that
take in more than just the dictates of universal [i.e., Kantian]
morality."[47] He believes, however, that "[t]ying the defense of
liberalism to so controversial an ideal of the person [as Kant's]
was a very shaky tactic" (70). Larmore himself prefers to draw
the distinction between *citoyen*, on the one hand, and *bourgeois*
or *homme*, on the other, with the result that

> [t]his does not mean that our highest personal ideal must be to
> conceive of ourselves as prior to our ends, without any constitu-
> tive attachment to a conception of the good. It means, instead,
> that the political system *treats* persons as not necessarily tied to
> any particular conception of the good, that is, apart from status
> and ascription (125).

His claim that "only a modus vivendi conception of justice"
makes intelligible the "sort of institutionalized myopia" (125)
underlying the *citoyen-homme* distinction will receive further
consideration in the next chapter.

Rawls's version of political liberalism, like that of Larmore, relies upon the distinction between the public, political domain of the *citoyen* and the private, associational domain of the *homme*. With respect to the former domain and its "political conception of the person," the operative conception is that of the individual as not defined or constituted by a factual-normative human *telos* (or by any other conception of the good to which he [contingently] adheres):

> As free persons, citizens claim the right to view their persons as independent from and not identified with any particular such conception [of the good] with its scheme of final ends. Given their moral power to form, revise, and rationally pursue a conception of the good, their public identity as free persons is not affected by changes over time in their determinate conception of it.[48]

The result is that, within a liberal democratic form of polity, "[c]laims that citizens regard as founded on duties and obligations based on their conception of the good and the moral doctrine they affirm in their own life are also, for our purposes here, to be counted as self-authenticating" (32). The idea behind this Rawlsian notion of citizens as "self-authenticating sources of valid claims" (33) is the following: Conceptions of the human good or *telos* affirmed by individual citizens (at least the reasonable ones allowed by a supposedly conceptually prior doctrine of the right or justice) are due whatever consideration they should receive from the government and from other citizens not because of the truth or cognitive content of those conceptions but simply because of the fact that they are affirmed by some free and equal citizens.

There is, then, a prominent tendency within liberalism to repudiate or adopt a position of skepticism toward the idea of a factual-normative human *telos*, which has sociopolitical consequences for the *citoyen* as well as private ones for the *homme*. An important difference among liberal theorists, however, pertains to the depth of this repudiation or skepticism. Those who might be grouped under the rubric of political liberalism typically profess themselves to be satisfied with a relatively shallow (or thin, to use an alternative metaphor) justification for tolerating alternative conceptions of the good. This toleration is to be limited to the political sphere, to the treatment persons receive as *citoyens*, and consequently need not be founded on any very deep moral, philosophical, or religious conception of the person. On the other hand, adherents to perfectionist liberalism typically insist that the full moral force of liberalism can be adequately explained and justified only by appeal to some fundamental assumptions concerning what human dispositions and attributes should, in a morally normative sense of 'should', be fostered by political institutions. Contemporary perfectionist liberals, in other words, profess skepticism with respect to the conviction that true political neutrality with respect to conceptions of the good can be maintained within a political philosophy of liberal democracy. I share this skepticism and attempt to elaborate it in the following section.

Stopping History and the Hunt for a *Tertium Quid*

Political liberalism is, in effect, committed to both (a) the construction of a justifying or legitimating theory in support of the principles, attitudes, and institutions of contemporary liberal democracy and (b) the attempt to make such a theory as neutral (and, thus, as widely acceptable) as possible by divorcing it from any deep religious, philosophical, or moral assumptions.

One way to achieve both desiderata is to embrace a conception of universal history according to which history ends with the production of liberal democratic forms of political organization. The idea (suggested by Kant and developed by Hegel and by Marx) is that natural processes, governed by laws that are in principle accessible to science, shape the development of institutions and principles of human sociopolitical cooperation into "a coherent and directional History of mankind."[49] Recently, Francis Fukuyama, influenced by the interpretation of Hegel by Alexandre Kojève,[50] has (re)entertained the hypothesis that this directional History (or "*Weltgeschichte* with a Big H," in Alan Ryan's memorable phrase[51]) "will eventually lead the greater part of humanity to liberal democracy."[52] Of course, the end of history in this sense does not mean that things stop happening or that something like the normal vicissitudes of social and political life cease. Rather, it means "that there would be no further progress in the development of the underlying principles and institutions, because all the really big questions [with respect to sociopolitical organization, that is] had been settled" (xii). Fukuyama begins with what is probably the widely held current view that "liberal democracy remains the only coherent political aspiration that spans different regions and cultures around the globe, (xiii), and concludes, tentatively, that the reason for the prevalence of this view is not simply lack of intellectual imagination but the Historical fact that development of human sociopolitical organization, in its broad outlines, has reached its natural culmination. An aspect of Fukuyama's book that seems to have been especially irritating to his critics is the similar suggestion he makes concerning "liberal principles in economics—the 'free market'" (xiii).

Part of the appeal of such a view is that it supplies a justification or grounding of liberal principles, attitudes, and institutions that is value-neutral, in a sense: It does not rest on openly normative religious, philosophical, or moral assumptions but on apparently factual claims about the development of human sociopolitical organization. Its motivating spirit is, in part, similar to the nineteenth-century scientism that led Marx to repudiate normative utopian socialism in favor of the dialectical, historical materialism that would culminate not in liberal polity but in the withered-away state of fully developed communism.

Marxist thought, in fact, raises one problem with the attempt to use History to justify liberal principles and polity. Even if *Weltgeschichte* (world History "with a Big H") does have a direction and a sociopolitical culmination or *telos*, it is far from obvious that liberalism represents that culmination. Marx, of course, had very different ideas on the subject. Most contemporary theorists of political liberalism, however, have deeper objections to this employment of universal History. These theorists represent, by and large, the English-language, analytic tradition of philosophy—or political theory heavily influenced by this philosophical tradition. Adherents to this tradition have generally been more skeptical than their European, continental counterparts about engaging in largely a priori speculation about what seem to be empirical matters—e.g., the course and end of History.

Similar strictures against moral theorizing decidedly do not

apply within the tradition shared by most contemporary theorists of political liberalism. Moreover, one suspects that, at least
in their heart of hearts, many such theorists share an attitude
described by Fukuyama:

> We, who live in stable, long-standing liberal democracies face an
> unusual situation. In our grandparents' time, many reasonable
> people could foresee a radiant socialist future in which private
> property and capitalism had been abolished, and in which poli-
> tics itself was somehow overcome. Today, by contrast, we have
> trouble imagining a world that is radically better than our own,
> or a future that is not essentially democratic and capitalist. Within
> that framework, of course, many things could be improved: we
> could house the homeless, guarantee opportunity for minorities
> and women, improve competitiveness, and create new jobs. We
> can also imagine future worlds that are significantly worse than
> what we know now, in which national, racial, or religious intoler-
> ance makes a comeback, or in which we are overwhelmed by war
> or environmental collapse. But we cannot picture to ourselves a
> world that is *essentially* different from the present one, and at the
> same time better. Other, less reflective ages also thought of them-
> selves as the best, but we arrive at this conclusion exhausted, as it
> were, from the pursuit of alternatives we felt *had* to be better than
> liberal democracy (46).

In brief, the intellectual tradition shared by most liberal democratic theorists does not give them the confidence to declare,
as a (quasi-)empirical fact, that History is ended. But, on the
other hand, most would very much like to Stop History. They
would like to construct a political theory that would serve the
dual functions (i) of *justifying* or *legitimating*, in some moral or
normative manner, some set of liberal principles, attitudes, and
institutions and (ii) of *stabilizing* or *entrenching* these principles,
attitudes, and institutions. Indeed, the construction of a theory
that would adequately serve these two functions represents the
preeminent contemporary liberal conception of what political
theory is all about.

A fundamental—but eminently questionable—assumption of
much of contemporary political liberalism is that the stabilizing and entrenching function (ii) can be accomplished by means
of or through the justifying and legitimating function (i).[53] As I
argued earlier, where the object of stabilization and entrenchment is a compromise or modus vivendi—really, a number of

compromises or piecemeal modi vivendi—an attempt at theoretical justification is apt to prove more controversial than what it is supposed to justify. To consider a somewhat more concrete case than I have thus far done, consider citizen *A* (myself, for example), who does not have any 'deep' moral objections to capital punishment. Citizen *A*, however, may be induced to join in a concerted political effort to abolish capital punishment because of what he deems to be the balance of various consequentialist considerations. Perhaps there is considerable evidence that sentences of capital punishment are applied in a discriminatory manner and that such sentences are more costly to the judiciary and penal system than sentences of life imprisonment, and not much evidence that the threat of capital punishment is an especially effective deterrent. Suppose, however, that the leaders of the movement against capital punishment present as the theoretical justification of their efforts some doctrine that capital punishment is invariably an violation of fundamental rights (natural or otherwise) of the person, or a violation of some basic principle of justice, or that it is cruel and unusual punishment, in the American constitutional sense of the phrase. Moreover, these leaders agitate for the *public* recognition of such grounds for abolition. Citizen *A* may well decide to withhold support from the movement, to withdraw from the compromise, rather than to be put in a position of recognizing, or appearing to recognize, what he deems to be fundamentally false moral principles—particularly if he thinks it possible that those principles will be applied in other areas to morally pernicious effect.

However, few contemporary theorists of political liberalism have been willing to forgo the attempt to provide theoretical justification for such items of liberal compromise as the stance of political neutrality with respect to conceptions of the good—even in the absence of any very cogent argument that such theoretical justification actually is, or could be, an efficient means for producing civil stability. Later and at greater length, I shall argue that this reluctance to give up the enterprise of *public* justification is regarded by liberal theorists as much more a matter of morality than of prudence. More specifically, a distinctively liberal conception of the nature of the person (or, at least, of the person *qua* citizen), plus a doctrine of political authority as devolving equally from individual citizens, mandates that any fundamental political matter must be justifiable, in a suitably idealized and theoretical sense, to each citizen.

The political liberal finds that he or she cannot rely simply on whatever might happen to be the outcome of actual, concrete political compromise, despite the fact that liberal historiography typically represents such compromise as the post-Reformation, early-Modern source of various aspects of liberal polity. For one thing, such compromises, if unconstrained, might yield illiberal results. But, even more important, liberal moral commitments demand an ideally universal justifiability that would entail some theoretical grounding of the fundamentals of liberal polity. However, the principles of political liberalism (as opposed to perfectionist liberalism) preclude appeal to a comprehensive conception of the good as the basis of theoretical justification of liberal modi vivendi. The result is the search for a *tertium quid*—a theoretical justification of fundamental items of liberal polity: something between the nonjustification of simply resting content with whatever the rough-and-tumble of concrete political compromise yields in particular issues and the appeal to a particular religious, philosophical, or moral doctrine (i.e., a Rawlsian comprehensive conception of the good).

The tactic of most political liberals has been to attempt to mark out this *tertium quid* with such adjectives as public and political—hence the term "*political* liberalism" for this particular contemporary tradition. Appeal is made to such notions as "public political culture of a democratic society" and a "public basis of justification" (Rawls[54]), "public reason" and a "political conception of the person" (Rawls), "public reasonableness" and "liberal public justification" (Macedo), "ideally rational conditions of [political] dialogue" or "norms of rational [political] argument" (Habermas, Larmore). The assumption is that this *tertium quid* of the public and political can serve a number of functions. (1) It can provide a principled, *moral* justification and legitimation of the fundamentals ("constitutional essentials and issues of basic justice" in Rawls's oft-used phrase) of liberal polity. (2) It can effect the stability and entrenchment of liberal political institutions and principles that political liberals apparently desire to achieve. (3) As a matter of moral right, it can win acceptance by all sufficiently rational citizens, irrespective of their private religious, moral, or philosophical commitments (comprehensive conceptions of the good) as long as those commitments are rational and reasonable ones. (4) And, finally, it can provide a sufficiently rich body of theoretical political doctrine to guide future political consideration and decisions concerning fundamental political matters.

I shall argue that such a *tertium quid* is not to be found—particularly considering how much political liberalism asks of it. Any conceptual framework that would provide for the *exis-tence* of such a neutral but morally normative patch of ground will certainly depend upon philosophical (or religious or moral) assumptions that historically have been, and continue to be, controversial.

In fact, the conceptual instability of various contemporary attempts to stake out a political and public *tertium quid* is noteworthy: Such attempts waver between claims that are practical and prudential and those that are principled and theoretical. Of course, the details vary with the particular theory of political liberalism in question. Habermas and Larmore attempt to rely more on the practical notion of modus vivendi but ultimately are forced to appeal to moral principles that transcend the prudential in order to sustain the notion of a *public* justification of political liberalism. Macedo and Rawls are more willing to appeal, openly, to normative principles; but the very nature of political liberalism dictates that this appeal must be accommodated to the demands of ideally universal acceptability or justifiability.

Prudential Accommodation versus Public Justification

In the following chapters, I shall suggest that the best conceptual move for the liberal is to give up the notion of *public* theoretical justification. Of course, within the context of contemporary liberal democracies, the liberal is as legally entitled as anyone to form his or her own justifying theory and work, with like-minded individuals, to bring public institutions and practices into conformity with that theory. But the same is true, within that sociopolitical context, for a wide variety of "illiberal" political theories. For reasons internal to the tradition,

political liberalism has tended to regard its advocacy of a supposedly neutral (vis-à-vis comprehensive conceptions of the
good) but morally normative theory of public argument and
justification as a matter of staking out the morally high
ground—as the avoidance of petty partisanship and appeal only
to incontrovertible principles of reason and rationality. Such a
way of regarding political liberalism on the part of its adherents, although historically understandable, seems to me to be
quite illusory. In what follows, I shall generally support the
claim by Margaret Moore that "[l]iberalism is itself a conception of the good, on all fours with other conceptions of the
good, and deeply antithetical to many moral and religious conceptions."[55] What seems to me to be the fact of the matter—
which I have already stated and to which I shall return—is the
following: Within the context of contemporary Western democracies, all political theory is ultimately partisan.

    "Other conceptions" of the good "on all fours" with lib-
eralism's include, inter alia, that of Marxism, of various varieties of communitarian socialism, and of Catholic natural-law
theory. I would endorse some variant of the last of these and
would have no moral qualms about attempting to further its
aims, whether they are in conformity with theoretical liberalism or not, in the political and social realm. However, as I shall
further argue in chapter 4, it seems quite unlikely—at least
within the context of contemporary Western democracies such
as the United States—that natural-law theory could win sufficient support to become anything like an official or *public* political theory. What, then, do I, as a non-liberal theorist, advocate
by way of a *public* justifying/legitimating political theory? The
short answer to this question is "none." As I just asserted, within the pluralistic context of contemporary liberal democracies,
all political theory—for better or worse—will be partisan. In
my own case, I should prefer to see some liberal principles,
practices, and institutions go by the boards entirely, others I
am willing to endorse qualifiedly, and still others I am willing,
at least for the time being and under present circumstances, to
live with as a matter of avoiding the greater evil.

    In other words, I advocate a radically pragmatic, selective,
and qualified accommodation with the liberalism of contemporary Western democracies. Whether this stance itself deserves
to be characterized by the adjective "liberal" I do not regard

as a particularly important or interesting question. However, one salient feature of this stance is that it is a matter of prudential public attitude rather than of a public justifying/ legitimating theory. Indeed, I make bold to suggest that such a radically prudential, pragmatic stance can serve as an attractive alternative to a liberal justifying/legitimating theory for citizens—nonliberal as well as liberal—within contemporary Western democracies. A point to which I shall return in chapter 4 is that such a pragmatic public attitude would seem to provide a considerably stronger endorsement of the institutional and procedural in Western democratic culture than of the conceptual and the substantive in the liberal intellectual tradition. In other words, the pragmatic public attitude that I recommend is quite thin and minimalist—perhaps too thin and minimalist to be attractive to the committed theoretical liberal. Yet I believe that it can provide a political umbrella that is, in certain ways, more capacious than any offered by the various versions of theoretical liberalism with which I am familiar. This pragmatic public attitude would at most entail a quite qualified, selective, and minimalist endorsement of elements of contemporary liberal polity. However, as I shall argue in chapter 3, the substitution of this pragmatic stance for the elusive neutral justifying liberal theory sought by political liberalism does not seem to be very directly relevant to the issue of the stability of contemporary constitutional democratic regimes.

Notes

1. Francis Fukuyama, *The End of History and the Last Man* (New York: The Free Press, 1992), 42.

2. John Rawls, *Political Liberalism*, The John Dewey Essays in Philosophy, no. 4 (New York: Columbia University Press, 1993), xix.

3. Ibid., xxii-xxiv.

4. Ibid., 159.

5. Fukuyama, 60.

6. Rawls, *Political Liberalism*, 159.

7. Will Kymlicka, *Liberalism, Community, and Culture* (Oxford: Clarendon Press, 1989), 33.

8. John Locke, *Epistola de Tolerantia, A Letter on Toleration*, ed. Raymond Klibansky (Oxford: Clarendon Press, 1968), 70.

9. Locke, *Second Treatise of Government*, ed. C. B. Macpherson (Indianapolis, Ind.: Hackett Publishing Company, Inc., 1980), chap. 2, 9.

10. Locke, *de Tolerantia*, 70.

11. Ibid., 64.

12. Raymond Klibansky, introduction to *Epistola de Tolerantia, A Letter on Toleration*, by John Locke, 24.

13. His inclusion of Moslems and Jews under the umbrella of toleration, however, probably went beyond the sort of consensus that many Protestants were willing to accept.

14. Locke, *de Tolerantia*, 132.

15. Ibid., 134.

16. John Locke, *An Essay concerning Human Understanding*, ed. Peter H. Nidditch (Oxford: Clarendon Press, 1975), bk. 4, chap. 3, 549.

17. Fukuyama, 60.

18. Aristotle, *Ethica Nicomachea*, ed. I. Bywater (Oxford: Clarendon Press, 1962), 6.2.1139a21–31.

19. Alasdair MacIntyre, *After Virtue: A Study in Moral Theory* (Notre Dame, Ind.: University of Notre Dame Press, 1981), 50.

20. Immanuel Kant, *Critique of Practical Reason*, trans. Lewis White Beck (Indianapolis, Ind.: The Bobbs-Merrill Company, Inc., 1956), 27 (vol. 5, 28). (For references to Kant I add, in parentheses, the volume and page number of the relevant passage as it appears in the Prussian Academy edition of Kant's works.)

21. John Ladd, translator's introduction to *The Metaphysical Elements of Justice*, by Immanuel Kant (Indianapolis, Ind.: The Bobbs-Merrill Company, Inc., 1965), xix.

22. Kant, *Metaphysical Elements of Justice*, 34 (vol. 6, 230).

23. Kant, "On the Proverb: That May be True in Theory, But is of No Practical Use", in Immanuel Kant, *Perpetual Peace and Other Essays on Politics, History, and Morals*, trans. Ted Humphrey (Indianapolis, Ind.: Hackett Publishing Company, Inc., 1983), 78 (vol. 8, 298).

24. Kant, "Idea for a Universal History with a Cosmopolitan Intent", in *Perpetual Peace and Other Essays*, ed. Humphrey, 33 (vol. 8, 22).

25. Ibid., 15 (17).

26. Kant, "To Perpetual Peace, A Philosophical Sketch," in *Perpetual Peace and Other Essays*, trans. Humphrey, 112 (vol. 8, 349–50)

27. Charles E. Larmore, *Patterns of Moral Complexity* (Cambridge: Cambridge University Press, 1987), 92.

28. Desiderius Erasmus, *De libero arbitrio diatribe seu collatio*, trans. E. Gordon Rupp and A. N. Marlow, in *Luther and Erasmus: Free Will and Salvation*, Library of Christian Classics, vol. 17 (Philadelphia: Westminster Press, 1969), 37.

29. Martin Luther, *De servo arbitrio*, trans. Philip S. Watson and B. Drewery, in *Luther and Erasmus*, 108–109.

30. Voltaire, François Marie Arouet, *Voltaire: Philosophical Dictionary*, trans. Peter Gay (New York, Basic Books,1962), vol. 2, 487–89.

31. Michel de Montaigne, "Apologie de Raimond Sebond," in *Les Essais de Michel de Montaigne*, ed. Pierre Villey, trans. Donald M. Frame,

vol. 2 (Paris, Societe Francaise d'Editions Litteraires et Techniques, 1922), 238-39.

32. Avrum Stroll, "Scepticism and Religious Toleration," *History of Philosophy Quarterly* 5, no. 3 (1988): 225.

33. Ronald M. Dworkin, "Liberalism," in *A Matter of Principle* (Cambridge, Mass.: Harvard University Press, 1985), 203.

34. Dworkin, *Law's Empire* (Cambridge, Mass.: Belknap Press, 1986), 441, n. 19.

35. Kymlicka, *Liberalism, Community and Culture*, 10.

36. Ibid., 18.

37. Rawls, *Political Liberalism*, 58.

38. Ibid., 37.

39. Roberto Mangabeira Unger, *Knowledge and Politics* (New York: The Free Press, 1975), 39.

40. Ibid., 41.

41. Dworkin, *Law's Empire*, 441, n. 19.

42. Kymlicka, *Liberalism, Community, and Culture*, 10.

43. Rawls, *Political Liberalism*, 60.

44. Ibid., 59.

45. Larmore, *Patterns of Moral Complexity*, 43.

46. Kymlicka, *Liberalism, Community, and Culture*, 18, 19.

47. Larmore, *Patterns of Moral Complexity*, 70.

48. Rawls, *Political Liberalism*, 30.

49. Fukuyama, *The End of History*, xii.

50. Alexandre Kojève, *Introduction to the Reading of Hegel: Lectures on the Phenomenology of Spirit Assembled by Raymond Queneau*, ed. Allan Bloom, trans. James H. Nichols, Jr. (New York: Basic Books, 1969). This is an abridged translation of his *Introduction à lecture de Hegel* (1947).

51. Alan Ryan, "Professor Hegel Goes to Washington," *The New York Review of Books* 3, no. 6 (March 26, 1992): 7.

52. Fukuyama, *The End of History*, xii.

53. Stephen Macedo recognizes the possible conflict between functions (i) and (ii). Admitting that "[p]ublic justification is not the only means of getting people to be liberals," he allows that there might be a "trade-off between candid public argument [i.e., attempted theoretical justification] and liberal socialization [i.e., getting people to go along with various liberal *modi vivendi*]" (*Liberal Virtues: Citizenship, Virtue, and Community in Liberal Constitutionalism* [Oxford: Clarendon Press, 1990], 64-65). With some qualifications that I find unclear and ambivalent (although public justification "should be compromised on none but the most pressing grounds . . . [w]e should be extremely reluctant to go further and avoid articulating what appear to be inescapable but possible divisive implications of liberalism" [69]), Macedo claims that his "own disposition is to adopt the public conception of justification and to deploy it candidly" (ibid.). Macedo's endorsement of this "disposition" seems to rest on grounds that are essentially moral. Much of the

apparent ambivalence that afflicts his discussion of this issue derives from tension between the pragmatic (prudential) and the principled (moral, theoretical) underpinnings of liberal modi vivendi, a tension to which I shall return in the text.

54. Rawls, *Political Liberalism*, 24–25, n. 27.

55. Margaret Moore, *Foundations of Liberalism* (Oxford: Clarendon Press, 1993), 177.

Chapter 2

What Ever Happened to Distributive Justice?

According to a classical Western preliberal tradition, the pre-eminent foundational virtue of political organization is distributive justice (*to neme tikon dikaion* in Aristotle's Greek, *iustitia distributiva* in St. Thomas Aquinas's Latin). It is characterized by Aristotle as being concerned "with the distribution of honors, money, and all the other things that are to be partitioned among those sharing in the civil polity (for in these matters it is possible for one to be either unequal or equal to another)."[1] The sort of equality involved in distributive justice, Aristotle says, is "proportionate" (*analogon*). That is, distributive shares should not necessarily be absolutely equal but, rather, proportionate to worth or merit: "[A]ll agree that what is just in matters of distribution must be according to merit of some kind (*kat' axian tina*); yet they do not mean the same thing by 'merit', but democrats mean status as freemen, oligarchs mean wealth, and aristocrats mean excellence."[2] Although it was Aristotle who introduced the terminology of distributive justice, it is clear that it represents essentially the same idea as Plato's account, in the *Republic*, of justice (*dikaiosune*) as each doing the "one thing with respect to the *polis* for which his nature has most fitted him" and each "keeping to his own with respect to having and doing."[3] In Aristotelian terminology, the idea is that justice requires a person's social status and function to be "proportional" (in a quasi-metaphorical sense of the term, of course) to his or her nature, talents, and abilities. St. Thomas Aquinas makes explicit the connection he sees between the Platonic and Aristotelian accounts: "[N]ow that is said to be 'each person's own' which is due to him according to equality of proportion. Therefore, the proper act of justice is nothing other than to render to each one what is his own."[4]

Of course, such accounts of distributive justice are, in themselves, extraordinarily schematic—that is to say, without content. They do not tell us *what* is to be distributed—goods or material welfare, in general, social status or prestige, respect or honor, sociopolitical duties, offices, or rights. And they do not tell us what relevant characteristics (of those to whom distribution is to be made) are to be invoked in order to effect the distribution in such a way that proportional equality is maintained. Common sense suggests that *different* characteristics might reasonably be invoked depending on whether what is being distributed is material goods, medical care, education, political functions or offices, occupations, or respect. Furthermore, it is far from obvious which such distributions should be held to be distinctively *political*, as opposed to matters more correctly left to the workings of other natural or conventional social mechanisms.

In other words, invocation of the notion of distributive justice as fundamental to political matters does not in itself really answer many substantive questions, even about the general form that political organization should take. Like many other abstract but fundamental moral concepts, it simply helps to provide a conceptual framework—a way of considering a range of sociopolitical issues. At a very schematic level, it is the conception of a shared human *telos*, Alasdair MacIntyre's man-as-he-could-be-if-he-realised-his-essential-nature, that makes possible an egalitarian application of the concept of distributive justice. That is, if all members of the community equally share in this quasi-factual, normative *telos*, then appeal might be made to the classical notion of distributive justice in order to argue that the sociopolitical means for instantiating or attaining this *telos* ought to be equally distributed. Of course, the notion of a human *telos* that is, in some sense, our common inheritance does not necessarily have egalitarian consequences. If (a) persons significantly differ in terms of their natural capacity for attaining such a *telos* and (b) what is relevant to the distribution of resources is the strength of such capacity, rather than the bare possession of the *telos* in question, then the proportional equality of distributive justice will demand that those with greater capacity for attaining our shared human *te-los* receive greater resources (or the appropriate *kind* of resources) for attaining it. This, in effect, is how distributive justice functions in Plato's *Republic*. The elaborate educational structure that Plato envisions sorts citizens in such a way that those who have the greater capacity for attaining the human *telos* of rationality—knowing the truth—are given the appropriate resources while those who do not have such capacity—those who are ultimately motivated by acquisitive appetites (*epithumia*) or the desire for power-honor-respect (*thumos*)— are given resources, such as external rational guidance, for controlling and making the best out of their more defective human natures. Also, appeal to distributive justice *vis-à-vis* a shared *telos*, even if the assumption is *not* made that persons significantly differ in their capacity to realize that *telos*, does not necessarily have any egalitarian consequences concerning the sharing of political power or participating in the political decision-making process. Most ancients regarded political decision making as a sort of *technē*—a skill, craft, or kind of practical knowledge. And possession or exercise of such knowledge or ability need have little to do with human-nature-as-it-could-be-if-it-realised-its-*telos* or with an individual's capacity for living up to that nature.

A plausible case can be made that the assimilation of the concept of human-nature-as-it-could-be-if-it-realised-its-*telos* into the framework of orthodox Christian theology strengthened its egalitarian potential. Our shared human *telos* becomes focused on our supernatural end, as children of God and as coheirs of the divine family. Even on the part of thinkers (such as St. Thomas) who tended to separate our mortal, natural *telos* from our eternal, supernatural one, there is not a complete divorce or compartmentalization between the two. There is a sufficient separation, however, that empirical differences among persons— even with respect to intellect, will, respectability or character— need not really compromise the equal dignity bestowed upon us because of our supernatural vocation. The contemporary theologian Bernard Häring, in his widely used theology text *Das Gesetz Christi* (*The Law of Christ*), puts the point as follows:

> As presented in the *Reconstruction of the Social Order* (*Quadrag-esimo Anno*) the concept of social justice belongs to the juridical

order and is based on the law of nature. As such, it is not strictly a supernatural concept. But such a notion of social justice could not be formed by man in his present state without the revealed concepts of God and man. In this concept humanity looks on all its possessions as a trust from God and the human race itself as a family of many members in God's sight. In the sense of the *Reconstruction of the Social Order*, social justice far transcends the order or relation of "*do ut des*" (give and take [more literally: "I give in order that you should give"]) between individual and individual, between community and individual. It can be discerned only through the perspective of faith in God, the Giver of all earthly gifts and powers, the Father of all children of men. It is the familial justice of the children of God.[5]

Along similar lines, Jacques Maritain has developed an interpretation of the distributive justice mandated by natural law according to which historical progress in the discernment of the natural law "is linked to a progress of equality among men."[6] Although Maritain repudiates an "arithmetical equality, which excludes all differentiation and inequality and which would bring all human persons down to the same level" (36-37), he suggests that "progress in the consciousness of each one of us of our fundamental equality and of our communion in human nature" (37) would naturally lead (by a principle of distributive justice mandating equal treatment for equals) to an equal sharing in the 'fundamental rights' characteristic of contemporary Western constitutional democracies. In other words, an egalitarian sharing in certain fundamental rights and freedoms is a consequence of "that proportionate equality which justice causes to exist when it treats every one in the manner in which he deserves, and, above all, every man as a man."[7]

Of course, the sort of theological or supernatural egalitarianism implied by such applications of the principle of distributive justice *need* not have any very determinate consequences with respect to distribution of temporal goods, particularly political authority or power, if that counts as a "temporal good." As Michael Walzer notes, the application of the principle of distributive justice is "an example of a thick or maximalist morality," and he continues,

Any full account of how social goods ought to be distributed will display the features of moral maximalism: it will be idiomatic in its language, particularist in its cultural reference, and circumstantial in the two senses of that word: historically dependent and factually detailed. Its principles and procedures will have been worked out over a long period of time through complex social interactions.[8]

While the thickness of the principle of distributive justice, when it is actually embedded in a social and cultural context, is in Walzer's view a natural and appropriate feature of the principle, such thickness did not find similar approbation in the liberal tradition, committed as it generally has been to the development of a universalist, streamlined, thin theory of sociopolitical morality. The result, within the liberal tradition, typically was either the abandonment of the concept of distributive justice as foundational to sociopolitical morality or the retention of only a restricted, thin, and (most important) egalitarian version of the concept.

Hobbes's Impatience: The Replacement of Distributive by Commutative Justice

The same scholastic tradition deriving from Aristotle that supplies the concept of distributive justice also supplies the correlative concept of rectificatory or commutative justice (*to-diortho tikon dikaion*, in Aristotle's Greek, *iustitia commutativa*, in St. Thomas Aquinas's Latin), which has to do with "rectification with respect to transactions" between individuals.[9] Such "transactions" may be either voluntary (contractlike) or involuntary from the perspective of at least one of the participants (tortlike). In either case, the kind of equality required by commutative justice is, Aristotle says, absolute or "arithmetic"—i.e., involving equal exchange, compensation, or return. The general assumption within the classical tradition influenced by this distinction was that, while distributive justice is, in part, properly a public sociopolitical concern, commutative justice pertains primarily to agreements (and injuries due compensation) between private individuals.

In his *De cive*, however, Thomas Hobbes departs dramatically from this traditional understanding of the distinction:

The justice of actions is commonly distinguished into two kinds, commutative and distributive; the former whereof, they say, consists in the arithmetical, the latter in geometrical proportion; and that is conversant in exchanging, in buying, selling, borrowing, lending, location and conduction; and other acts whatsoever belonging to contractors; where, if there be an equal return made, hence, they say, springs commutative justice: but this is busied about the dignity and merits of men; so as if there be rendered to every man κατὰ τὴν ἀξίαν, more to him who is more worthy, and less to him that deserves less, and that proportionably; hence, they say, ariseth distributive justice. . . . But what is all this to justice? For neither if I sell my goods for as much as I can get for them, do I injure the buyer, who sought and desired them of me; neither if I divide more what is mine to him who deserves less, so long as I give the other what I have agreed for, do I wrong to either. Which truth our Saviour himself, being God, testifies in the Gospel. This therefore is no distinction of justice, but of equality. Yet perhaps it cannot be denied that justice is a certain equality, as consisting in this only; that since we are all equal by nature, one should not arrogate more right to himself than he grants to another, unless he have fairly gotten it by compact. And let this suffice to be spoken against this distinction of justice, although now almost generally received by all; lest any man should conceive an injury to be somewhat else than the breach of faith or contract, as hath been defined above.[10]

There is a note of exasperated impatience (not uncommon in Hobbes) in his dismissal of the notion of distributive justice, "busied," as it is, "about the dignity and merits of men." Human beings, in view of their psychological construction, cannot but disagree on such matters: "all controversies are bred from hence, that the opinions of men differ concerning *meum* and *tuum* [mine and thine], *just* and *unjust*, *profitable* and *unprofitable*, *good* and *evil*, *honest* and *dishonest*, and the like; which every man esteems according to his own judgment."[11] Consequently, says Hobbes,

[i]f nature therefore have made men equal, that equality is to be acknowledged; or if nature have made men unequal, yet because men that think themselves equal will not enter into conditions of peace but upon equal terms, such equality must be admitted. And therefore for the ninth law of nature, I put this: *that every man acknowledge another for his equal by nature*. The breach of this precept is *pride*.[12]

The "equality by nature" postulated by Hobbes, however, is of a very abstract and ideal kind:

> They are equals who can do equal things one against the other; but they who can do the greatest thing, namely, kill, can do equal things. All men therefore among themselves are by nature equal; the inequality we now discern, hath its spring from the civil law.[13]

The relevance of this minimal sort of equality to issues of distributive justice depends entirely on Hobbes's theoretical fiction of state of nature and social contract as an account of political authority: the supposedly equal vulnerability to harm makes the state of nature's *bellum omnium contra omnes* (war of each against all) equally insupportable (i.e., a state in which life is equally "solitary, poor, nasty, brutish, and short"[14]). It thus puts persons on an equal footing, at least with respect to motivation, for entering into the social contract by which the all-powerful Leviathan of civil polity is created. Of course, in actual life, people are not really equal even in this minimal sense: Some persons are more vulnerable than others and, indeed, much of the political and judicial machinery of society is designed to deal with this fact.

Hobbes, as well as other proponents of the social-contract tradition of early liberalism, sees actual human inequality as an artifact of civil law or, more broadly, that complex of social conventions, traditional and legal, that constitute human nurture as opposed to nature. But an irony of this tradition is that it is such egalitarian conceptions of human nature that smack of the artificial and the conventional. The social-contract tradition of classical liberalism has given up, or at least has begun to give up, on the teleological conception of human-nature-as-it-could-be-if-it-realised-its-*telos*, which had allowed an egalitarian application of the concept of distributive justice. What social-contract liberalism substitutes in its place is an egalitarian conception of socially-uncontaminated-human-nature-in-the-state-of-nature. Such a notion may seem, superficially at least, to be an empirical notion—more empirical, anyway, than the older factual-normative conception of human-nature-as-it-could-be-if-it-realised-its-*telos*. As the social-contract tradition matured, however, it was increasingly openly acknowledged that the state of nature is an ahistorical conceptual construct.

The problem, then, for contemporary liberal theorists is whether egalitarian assumptions about human beings (e.g., Rawls's political conception of persons as "free and equal") are (a) empirical claims about actual human beings as we find them, (b) the embodiment of deep religious, metaphysical, or moral commitments concerning the ultimate nature of persons (akin to the factual-normative notion of human-nature-as-it-could-be-if-it-realised-its-*telos*), or (c) merely representative of a necessary (or relatively more workable) dictate of political expediency, rather than any expression of truth—be it empirical, metaphysical, religious, or moral. Contemporary theorists of political liberalism have generally tended officially to eschew (b): Resting political equality on such a footing looks too much like an illicit privileging of a particular comprehensive conception of the good. Consequently, they have tended to waver between foundations (a) and (c)—between attempting to ground empirically egalitarian sociopolitical assumptions and attempting to argue for such egalitarian assumptions on grounds of pragmatic political expediency. I shall argue later in this chapter that neither attempt works. A foundation of type (b)—appeal to some deep, normative metaphysical or moral assumptions—is needed; and I shall suggest the most plausible place within the tradition of liberalism, classical and contemporary, in which to find it. Of course, such a move would contradict the stance of supposed neutrality at the center of the tradition of contemporary *political* liberalism.

It is arguable, however, that egalitarian assumptions concerning man in the state of nature did not actually do much work, *vis-à-vis* distributive justice, in one classical liberal tradition, a tradition that issued in contemporary libertarianism. It is clear that Hobbes, despite his endorsement of a sort of equality of persons in the state of nature, thinks that justice is really a matter of *commutative* justice. In the passage from *De cive* III, 6 quoted earlier, there is an important qualification—"unless he have fairly gotten it by compact"—to Hobbes's claim that the fact that we are "equal by nature" dictates that "one should not arrogate more right to himself than he grants to another." And, at the conclusion of this passage, he clearly states that the point of his attack on the traditional notion of distributive justice has been to forestall anyone from "conceiv[ing] an injury to be somewhat else than the breach of faith or contract."

The contractlike and tortlike issues comprehended by the notion of commutative justice are, it might seem, more straightforward and tractable than those controversial issues of distributive justice, which require us to busy ourselves "about the dignity and merits of men."

The idea that considerations of commutative justice, especially obligations devolving from contract or agreement, take precedence over considerations of distributive justice is by no means unique to Hobbes in the early history of liberal political theory. It is arguable that John Locke has a thicker conception of natural human equality—to which I shall shortly return—than does Hobbes. However, C. B. Macpherson has argued convincingly that Locke makes clever use of the notion of implicit contract to trump the egalitarian implications of his natural-right doctrine of property. In the fifth chapter of the *Second Treatise of Government*, Locke develops his famous doctrine of property: "God, who hath given the world to men in common, hath also given them reason to make use of it to the best advantage of life, and convenience."[15] Reason dictates that property, in order to be used, must be appropriated by the individual person from the common stock of nature. This is done by the individual's "mixing his labour" with what nature provides—e.g., by gathering, cultivating, harvesting, improving, etc. Two restrictions apply to property appropriation: (1) "enough, and as good" must be left for appropriation by others (sec. 27, 19); (2) one may not appropriate so much that it spoils, as "[n]othing was made by God for man to spoil or destroy" (sec. 31, 21). As Locke notes, such a doctrine justifies a quite limited acquisition and roughly egalitarian distribution of property.

The introduction of the use of money, however, legitimizes unequal property distribution. For money enables one to (1) acquire property (capital) in a form that does not entail spoilage, (2) mix not only his own personal labor, but also the labor that he buys, with nature in order to acquire property, and (3) leaves, by the increased efficiency of production that capital-acquisition yields, "enough, and as good" *produce* (if not land) for others. In summary, Locke writes,

> But since gold and silver, being little useful to the life of man in proportion to food, raiment, and carriage, has its *value* only from the consent of men, . . . it is plain, that men have agreed to a

disproportionate and unequal *possession of the earth*, they having, by a tacit and voluntary consent, found out a way how a man may fairly possess more land than he himself can use the product of, by receiving in exchange for the overplus gold and silver, which may be hoarded up without injury to any one; these metals not spoiling or decaying in the hands of the possessor (sec. 50, 29).

Positive law pertaining to property, then, simply regulates the terms of exchange and unequal property distribution to which we have implicitly consented by the use of money.

Macpherson, in a passage of some irony, compliments Locke's achievement:

> As a liberal ideology it has almost everything that could be desired. It starts with free and equal individuals none of whom have any claim to jurisdiction over others: this is a characteristic and essential assumption of the proponents of a liberal as opposed to a feudal or patriarchal or absolutist state. It acknowledges that these individuals are self-interested and contentious enough to need a powerful state to keep them in order, but it avoids the Hobbesian conclusion that the state must have absolute and irrevocable power: . . . . Moreover, Locke makes a unique and ingenious case for a natural right of unlimited private property, with which society and government are not entitled to interfere: no-one, before or since, has come near his skill in moving from a limited and equal to an unlimited and unequal property right by invoking rationality and consent.
>
> The confluence of his main lines of argument about government and property right provides an eminently useable ideological underpinning for the modern liberal capitalist state.[16]

The conceptual move alluded to by Macpherson here, "invoking rationality and consent," is indeed central to the liberal tradition of political thought. Historically, it is involved with the privileging of considerations of commutative justice, especially those concerned with contracts and contractlike matters, over considerations of distributive justice.

This particular aspect of classical liberalism, with its tendency to privilege commutative over distributive justice, is particularly emphasized in the contemporary *libertarian* tradition. This point has been made by Rawls, in somewhat different terminology, in his recent book *Political Liberalism*. According to the standard libertarian conception the legitimate functions of a minimal state, "protection against force, theft, fraud, enforcement of contracts, and so on,"[17] pertain to just those contract-like and tortlike matters that fall within the scope of commutative/rectificatory justice. Rawls characterizes the program of libertarianism as an attempt "to see how the minimal state could have arisen from a perfectly just situation by a series of steps each of which is morally permissible and violates no one's rights" (263). The idea—certainly redolent of Hobbes, of Locke, and of contractarianism, in general—is to begin with a "distributively just" state-of-nature or other "initial position" and then, in effect, let only commutative justice be invoked to define sociopolitical justice thereafter. Rawls maintains, however, that libertarianism "is not a *social* contract theory at all" because, in his view, the social contract should be viewed "as establishing a system of common public law which defines and regulates political authority and applies to everyone as citizen" (265). That is, when Rawls claims that libertarianism "has no place for a special theory of justice for the basic structure" (265), he is really complaining of its lack of a substantive account of *distributive* justice for the sociopolitical sphere.

Locke's Ambivalence: Principle or Prudence?

Liberalism, in contrast to libertarianism, is generally committed to retaining some egalitarian conception of distributive justice as a fundamental controlling principle of the sociopolitical order. Although John Locke may be prepared to go some distance with Hobbes (and later libertarians) in sacrificing distributive to commutative justice, concern with distributive justice is certainly not absent from his political theory. There exists, however, a deep ambiguity in his account of the *basis* of the equality enjoined by his version of distributive justice. This ambiguity, which he perhaps inherits from the Anglican theologian Richard Hooker, is magnificently displayed in a passage from Hooker's *Of the Laws of Ecclesiastical Polity* quoted by Locke in the second chapter of the *Second Treatise of Government*. After commenting on the centrality of "[t]his *equality* by nature" to Hooker's moral theory, Locke quotes directly from the first book of *Ecclesiastical Polity*:

The like natural inducement hath brought men to know that it is
no less their duty, to love others than themselves; for seeing those
things which are equal, must needs all have one measure; if I cannot but wish to receive good, even as much at every man's hands,
as any man can wish unto his own soul, how should I look to
have any part of my desire satisfied, unless myself be careful to
satisfy the like desire, which undoubtedly is other men, being of
one and the same nature? To have any thing offered them repug-
nant to this desire, must needs in all respects grieve them as much
as me; so that if I do harm, I must look to suffer, there being no
reason that others should shew greater measure of love to me, than
they have by me shewed unto them: my desire therefore to be
loved of my equals in nature, as much as possibly may be,
imposeth upon me a natural duty of bearing to them-ward
fully the like affection; from which relation of equality between
ourselves and them that are as ourselves, what several rules and
cannons natural reason hath drawn, for direction of life, no man
is ignorant.[18]

It is obvious that Hooker and Locke (as well as Hobbes) make
a principle of reciprocity—the Golden Rule, "*do ut des* (give and
take)", or "*quod tibi fieri non vis, alteri ne feceris* (you should
not do to others what you do not wish to be done to your-
self)"—central to their conceptions of natural law. It is also
obvious that one construal of such a principle by Hooker (and
by Hobbes and Locke) is essentially pragmatic or prudential:
When one finds oneself in a social context with others who are,
in the jargon of contemporary political theory, "symmetrically
situated" (that is, we mutually recognize each other to be
roughly similarly psychologically motivated and roughly equal
in abilities, power, etc.), it makes good prudential sense, in furthering one's own private interests and goals, to accept some
such principle of reciprocity in the application of which one
treats others as equal to oneself in terms of their interests, goals,
desire for respect, 'having a say' in any joint action that we
may undertake, etc. Of course, in contexts where one does *not*
assume that others are relevantly symmetrically situated, one
may not have any reason to accept or act on a principle of reciprocity that embeds an equality assumption.

The other construal of the principle is, as it were, theoretical rather than practical: "those things that are equal, must
needs all have one measure" (chap. 2, sec. 5). The fact that
human beings are "creatures of the same species and rank,

promiscuously born to all the same advantages of nature"[19] dictates, by egalitarian application of the concept of distributive justice, that they should receive equal political treatment. And this principle holds irrespective of any personal advantage I hope to derive from treating others as my equals and irrespective of whether they adopt the same stance toward me. Locke grounds his 'principled' or theoretical egalitarian version of distributive justice in a characteristic Protestant theodicy. Human persons are, individually, the "workmanship of one omnipotent, and infinitely wise creator" and

> servants of one master, sent into the world by his order, and about his business; they are his property, whose workmanship they are, made to last during his, not one another's pleasure: and being furnished with like faculties, there cannot be supposed any such *subordination* among us, that may authorize us to destroy one another, as if we were made for one another's uses, as the inferior ranks of creatures are for our's.[20]

In other words, Locke grounds his egalitarianism, as well as many of the liberal freedoms, in a privatized conception of vocation. Each of us is sent into the world on an individual mission by God, which will contribute decisively to our supernatural destiny; and this vocation is, in each person's case, the exclusive business of that person and God. Interference from Throne or Altar, beyond what is required for maintaining decency and public order and protecting the property of individuals, is to be deprecated and resisted.

I conjecture that the ambiguity between the prudential, "*do ut des*" and the principled, religious-metaphysical foundations for Locke's egalitarian conception of distributive justice was not really regarded as an ambiguity by him. In the light of his hedonistic theory of action, on the one hand, and his rationalizing conception of morality and religion, on the other, the two foundations simply represent two necessary components of any account of moral *practice*. The latter principled, theologico-metaphysical account provides the rational justification for egalitarian application of a concept of distributive justice; the former prudential, "*do ut des*" account provides the motivational impetus necessary to elicit action in conformity with such a conception. However, the two accounts do not fit together so well in other conceptual frameworks. And in the later history of liberal political theory, they often represent *alternative*, and perhaps inconsistent, approaches to the justification of egalitarian forms of distributive justice.

We find ourselves with the three choices, previously outlined, concerning the basis of egalitarian distributive justice: (a) empirical generalizations about people as we actually find them, (b) religious-metaphysical-moral commitments concerning the fundamental nature of persons, and (c) sociopolitical prudence or expediency. For reasons that we have examined and to which we shall return, choice (b) is suspect from the viewpoint of contemporary political liberalism, which leaves choices (a) and (c). We have seen that Locke's doctrine of human action makes it natural for him to embrace the prudential choice (c). And perhaps there is also the occasional suggestion of the 'empirical equality' of persons although such a suggestion never appears in anything but a supporting role. The religious-metaphysical choice (b) is crucial to Locke's support of egalitarian distributive justice, but he scarcely qualifies as a *political* liberal, in the contemporary sense of this phrase. Theoretical liberalism requires some deep religious-metaphysical-moral foundation for the egalitarian form of distributive justice to which it is committed. Pragmatic or prudential grounds (c) and empirical considerations (a) are not enough to get what liberalism wants by way of egalitarianism. But, as theorists of political liberalism have recognized, reliance on a religious-metaphysical-moral foundation of type (b) ill accords with both contemporary liberalism's own historiography of its development and purpose and the particular approach it has taken to stopping History by means of supposedly neutral 'public' justification/legitimation.

Why Not Egalitarianism as a Prudential Modus Vivendi?

There are really two sorts of prudential or pragmatic arguments found in the literature of contemporary liberal theory for egalitarian application of a concept of distributive justice. One is of a rough-and-ready empirical sort. Contemporary Western sociopolitical culture (which is typically taken to be spreading to the rest of the world as well) simply will not sit back and peacefully tolerate anything less than an egalitarian version of distributive justice regarding such fundamental sociopolitical "goods" as participation in political decision-making processes, certain civil and human liberties, and neutral toleration of a range of life-styles or comprehensive conceptions of the good). The second is a rather more rarified, game-theoretical elaboration of the first. The dictates of practical rationality yield strategies of reciprocity that are essentially egalitarian in import, particularly in contemporary Western sociopolitical culture, inhabited by symmetrically situated free and equal citizens with a diversity of attachments that might be termed "self-interested" (at least in the sense that they are regarded as matters of personal, individual conviction). The practically rational citizen will recognize that the most effective way of pursuing his own comprehensive conception of the good is to adopt strategies of reciprocity based on egalitarian assumptions about the distribution of fundamental sociopolitical goods such as those listed above.

The former, empirical sort of prudential argument must, of course, depend on empirical assumptions, and these are typically open to doubt. Rawls, for example, writes of the necessity of our "recogniz[ing] the practical impossibility of reaching reasonable and workable political agreement in judgment on truth of comprehensive doctrines, especially an agreement that might serve the political purpose, say, of achieving peace and concord in a society characterized by religious and philosophical difference."[21] Elsewhere, he presents as a "fact about the public culture of a constitutional regime" that the diversity due to "reasonable pluralism" "can be overcome only by the oppressive use of state power."[22] What is suggested by Rawls and other political liberals but perhaps not always explicitly stated is that the "public culture of a constitutional regime" presents us with an *empirical* exhaustive disjunction: either we adopt some generic form of liberalism (with its officially egalitarian distribution of civil and human rights, its stance of neutrality with respect to 'reasonable' conceptions of the good, and its supposedly neutral, public justifying theory) *or* we shall face massive dissent and civil disorder that could be controlled only by secret police, torture cells, and jackbooted soldiery. Political history suggests that such an empirical disjunction is not ex-

haustive. State power—force or the threat of force—is a necessary constituent of any form of polity and it is certainly evident in liberal constitutional democracies: it might even be
termed "oppressive" where legally binding decisions are taken
than impinge upon citizens' fundamental values (comprehensive conceptions of the good). Of course, what leads to civil
disorder and what counts as oppressive are, in fact, largely
matters of perception. And perception is, in part, culturally and
educationally determined, susceptible to control by effective
public relations campaigns, among other factors. What would
be perceived as oppressive use of state power differs in, say,
the United States, Germany, Japan, and Singapore. Even recent
history shows that within any one of these contemporary "first-
world" states (e.g., the United States) such perceptions are quite
malleable and can undergo rather rapid transformation.

Upon reflection it will become evident that any effective
prudential or pragmatic grounding of liberalism's egalitarian
notion of distributive justice must move to the second, more
game-theoretical sort of argument. When we imagine symmetrically situated agents, each wishing to advance his own interests or comprehensive conception of the good, an appropriate
conception of practical reason will dictate that such agents accept principles of distributive justice of an egalitarian variety:
That is, each will allot to all equal liberties and other sociopolitical goods that are being distributed. It is this tradition that
has produced some of the most technical and influential work
within contemporary sociopolitical thought. I do not propose
to engage in a detailed review of this literature. There is, however, a general problem with the employment of prudential,
game-theoretical arguments for egalitarian principles of distributive justice. The agents constituting a postulated sociopolitical set-up typically must be symmetrically situated with none
having an advantage relative to the others in the bargaining
situation and, more generally, all being attributed such characteristics that make it rational for each individual not to distinguish between his own interest and that of any other arbitrarily
selected agent. In other words (as Rousseau puts it), the symmetry among individuals must be such that "there is no one
who does not take that word 'each' to pertain to himself and
in voting for all think of himself."[23] In actual, concrete sociopolitical situations, however, persons are not symmetrically situ-

ated sufficiently for *actual* prudential, self-interested practical rationality to yield this consequence. For the argument to work, one must either assume very idealized fictionalized agents or invoke a very idealized conception of practical rationality. In either case, it is no longer clear that the resulting argument, yielding egalitarian principles of distributive justice, has much relevance to what persons in concrete sociopolitical contexts would or should decide solely on the basis of prudential considerations. Two illustrations of such theoretical prudence-based arguments and their limitations may help concretize this point.

The first illustration is Rawls's now famous contractarian argument: the derivation of his two principles of "justice as fairness" by idealized agents in what he calls the "original position." In their more recent form, the two principles—"lexically ordered" (i.e., with the first taking priority over the second)—are as follows:

a. Each person has an equal claim to a fully adequate scheme of equal basic rights and liberties, which scheme is compatible with the same scheme for all; and in this scheme the equal political liberties, and only those liberties, are to be guaranteed their fair value.

b. Social and economic inequalities are to satisfy two conditions: first, they are to be attached to positions and offices open to all under conditions of fair equality of opportunity; and second, they are to be to the greatest benefit of the least advantaged members of society.[24]

As Rawls notes, these principles "express an egalitarian form of liberalism" (6). To make a rather long and complex story short, Rawls argues that appropriately rational and self-interested agents (or, more properly, agents that are rational and who are exclusively motivated by the interests of the persons whom they, individually, represent) would select the principles of justice as fairness as principles of evaluation of sociopolitical organization *if they were symmetrically situated in the original "bargaining" position.* In such a context, each agent would be able rationally to identify him- or herself (or the interest of the person represented) with the interest of any arbitrarily selected person among those being represented in the bargaining position. Thus he or she will select principles in conformity with a maximum strategy, seeking to make as good as possible the least advantaged positions in the sociopolitical set-up. Rawls realizes, however, that in order to achieve egalitarian liberal results his agents must be symmetrically situated. None may have any bargaining advantage; but they must also, by the Rawlsian "veil of ignorance," be deprived of information about the particulars of the sociopolitical milieu of the persons they represent and about the social position and comprehensive conception of the good of those persons. For example, were a party to the original position to know (a) that a particular religious doctrine were of the utmost importance to the person he represents and (b) that that doctrine was held by most persons in the sociopolitical milieu of the person he represents, the party in question might well not be eager to endorse a principle of 'liberty of conscience' and strict political neutrality with respect to religious matters.

The result is that Rawls cannot regard the derivation of his egalitarian principles of justice as an argument for those principles from prudential self-interest, i.e., as an argument that practical reason directed by prudential self-interest will dictate liberal egalitarian principles of distributive justice in real-world situations characterized by divergent interests and conceptions of the good. In fact, he does not regard his derivation in this way. As he has made increasingly clear, the derivation of his principles of justice by parties in the original position is to be regarded as a "device of representation" (24). A device to represent what? Rawls's considered answer seems to be a conception of distributive justice endemic to or, at least, widely held within the "public political culture of a [contemporary] democratic society" (13).

Rawls here encounters a fundamental problem with political liberalism. There may indeed be some such thing as the "public political culture of democratic society" containing, inter alia, some such widely held convictions about distributive justice as the importance of equal opportunity. But if there is such a conception, it will surely be rather amorphous and thin. It began, by liberalism's own favored historiography, in expediency as a compromise or modus vivendi, and will likely be accepted in a piecemeal fashion, under a variety of interpretations and for divergent reasons. The commitment of political liberalism to a 'public' justifying theory for what began as, and arguably still is, a compromise is in effect a request to accept more—and often at a deeper level of principle—than is contained in the compromise that supposedly is being justified.

Thus, the ignorance of the parties to Rawls's original position of the particular comprehensive conceptions of the good of the persons they represent constitutes something fundamental about Rawls's conception of the content of the notion of distributive justice implicit in the "public political culture of democratic society":

> [T]he fact that we affirm a particular religious, philosophical, or moral comprehensive doctrine with its associated conception of the good is not a reason for us to propose, or to expect others to accept, a conception of justice that favors those of that persuasion (24).

Perhaps the simple fact that I "affirm" a particular doctrine is not a reason to "propose, or expect others to accept, a conception of justice that favors those of that persuasion" (e.g., me). But if this claim is correct, it would seem to hold for any assertions: those of religion, philosophy, or morality, those of science and public policy, and those derived from Rawls's own conception of justice as fairness. It would also seem to be the case that the truth of an assertion (or one's conviction of the truth of such an assertion) is a good reason, although a defeasible one, for proposing it and for expecting others to accept it. And this is just as true for assertions representing comprehensive conceptions of the good, or assertions representing the aspects of such conceptions that impinge on issues of distributive justice, as it is for other scientific, moral, or political assertions.

Within the 'public' realm, Rawls and many other political liberals are committed to what I term the subjective stance with respect to religious, philosophical, or moral components of comprehensive doctrines. That is, they are committed to focusing on "the fact that we affirm" such a doctrine rather than on the cognitive content of such doctrines. Furthermore, they are committed to a conception of public action as "favor[ing] those of [a certain] persuasion" rather than as promoting the content of such a doctrine. The subjective stance is not assumed by Rawls with respect to issues falling under the rubric "right," in terms of the supposed antithesis of right and good. Nor is it assumed by him with respect to many other areas of science and public policy. Rawls (and other political liberals) may here invoke the liberal historiography of compromise and modus vivendi regarding "comprehensive doctrines" in order to justify this very selective application of the subjective stance. But, as I argue further in the next chapter, it appears that such a pragmatic justification of basic theoretical commitments is insufficient.

Such basic theoretical commitments as the right/good antithesis and selective application of the subjective stance are elements of Rawls's theory of public justification that are more controversial (and rightly so) than any thin conceptions of distributive justice that may be implicit in our "public political culture of democratic society." Rawls is thus put in the position of attempting to justify the relatively less controversial by the relatively more controversial—attempting to justify whatever develops by way of compromise or modus vivendi by fundamental philosophical and moral principles concerning which there is continuing controversy within contemporary democratic society. The situation is exacerbated by the special role accorded to political theory by political liberals: providing a public (and, hence, shared or shareable) justifying theory and, in so doing, stabilizing and entrenching liberal principles, policies, and institutions. More particularly, the political stance of neutrality regarding competing conceptions of the good has become orthodox doctrine within the tradition of political liberalism. But the case of Rawls suggests that the political liberal must appeal to philosophical and moral principles that must ultimately be regarded as components of comprehensive doctrines in order to stop History by stabilizing and entrenching liberal modi vivendi by means of public, justifying theory.

My second illustration of a prudence-based theoretical argument for a liberal egalitarian conception of distributive justice is Charles Larmore's version of the "ideal conversations" theory. As it turns out, Larmore, like Rawls, must ultimately rely on more than a prudentially based modus vivendi to obtain the egalitarian conception of distributive justice that he desires. Larmore is especially interested in the justification of political liberalism's stance of political neutrality with respect to conceptions of the good. The stance of neutrality may be regarded as the capstone of political liberalism's egalitarian conception of distributive justice: This conception of distributive justice mandates equal treatment of persons and requires equal respect for their conceptions of the good or comprehensive doctrines. And, according to most versions of political liberalism, such equal respect can be achieved only by the stance of political neutrality regarding comprehensive doctrines. But, as Larmore well realizes, political liberalism would thus seem to require "neutral justification of political neutrality."[25] What better place to look for such a neutral justification than to some prudential, pragmatic, or modus vivendi argument?

Larmore attempts to find neutral justification of political neutrality in a rational-dialogue model, which, as he says, owes much to the thought of Jürgen Habermas. Larmore invokes what he takes to be

> a universal norm of rational dialogue. When two people disagree about some specific point, but wish to continue talking about the more general problem they wish to solve, each should prescind from the beliefs that the other rejects, (1) in order to construct an argument on the basis of his other beliefs that will convince the other of the truth of the disputed belief, or (2) in order to shift to another aspect of the problem, where the possibilities of agreement seem greater. In the face of disagreement, those who wish to continue the conversation should retreat to *neutral ground*, with the hope of either resolving the dispute or of bypassing it (53).

This approach is prudentially based because of the assumption that individual self-interest or the pursuit of one's conception of the good makes social cooperation necessary or desirable. This general value of cooperation is the rationale for the desire to "continue the sociopolitical dialogue," to use the quasi-metaphorical language of the model. In order to continue the sociopolitical dialogue, practical rationality dictates that, in general, one make some egalitarian assumptions about the parties to the dialogue and, in particular, one adopt the stance of neutrality, described by Larmore, concerning what turns out to be controversial in the dialogue.

I return to some of the epistemic features of this picture of sociopolitical activity in the following chapter. For the moment, I wish to concentrate on one feature of the picture that is noted by Larmore himself: Although the rational-dialogue model of sociopolitical cooperation is, at its foundation, prudentially based, such a basis is insufficient for grounding an egalitarian stance of neutrality that is as inclusive and comprehensive as is desired by most liberals (evidently including Habermas and Larmore). As Larmore remarks, "[w]hen those with whom we are in disagreement have views for which we nonetheless feel some sympathy, or possess along with others who share their views some significant amount of power, the reasons for continuing the conversation are obvious" (59).

It is nonetheless true that Larmore's conception of liberal neutrality is more pragmatic, i.e., less deep and principled, than that of many other contemporary theorists of political liberalism. For example,

> [i]t does not require that the state be neutral with respect to all conceptions of the good life, but only with respect to those actually disputed in society. Where everyone agrees about some element of human flourishing, the liberal should have no reason to deny it a role in shaping political principle (67).

He remains sufficiently liberal, however, that he wishes to admit everyone—or at least even those who find themselves in very small minorities or are otherwise lacking in political clout—to egalitarian membership in the sociopolitical conversation club.

Ultimately, Larmore justifies the inclusion of parties to this club—including parties that need not be included because of prudential interest—on the grounds that we "wish to show everyone *equal respect*" (61). This sort of respect, as Larmore conceives it, is not a corollary of practical reason ("there is nothing contrary to reason in refusing to treat others as they treat us" [65]). Furthermore, it is a matter of respect for *persons*, not a matter of respect for or some degree of sympathy for *beliefs* or comprehensive doctrines held by persons:

> [R]espect for beliefs is not something that anyone can be expected to accord equally to all. Some beliefs deserve it, others do not. By contrast, a capacity for working out a coherent view of the

world is one that everyone (except some of the clinically insane) possesses. So respect for persons, as an attitude involving recognition of this capacity, is something that we can show equally to others. Of course, some people have this capacity to a greater degree than others do, but respect is something that others as persons are due just by virtue of having that capacity, so it should be given equally to all.

. . . . The *obligation* of equal respect consists in our being obligated to treat another as he is treating us—to use his having a perspective on the world as a reason for discussing the merits of our action rationally with him (in the light of how we understand a rational discussion). This is the way in which equal respect involves mutual respect, as Hegel understood (64-65).

Equal respect for persons, Larmore suggests, is based on something that seems to be, to some degree, an empirical characteristic of persons: the capacity for practical rationality, the "capacity for having a perspective on the world," or the "capacity for working out a coherent view of the world and indeed of the good life" (65).

That the possession of such a capacity should have the sociopolitical consequences that Larmore and other liberal theorists derive from it takes us beyond the empirical and, implicitly at least, must involve appeal to fundamental philosophical, moral, or religious assumptions. In particular, *egalitarian* claims concerning these consequences seem to involve a virtual nonsequitur. Larmore, in the passage just quoted, after admitting that "some people have this capacity [for "developing a coherent view of the world and indeed of the good life] to a greater degree than others do," proceeds to assert that "respect is something that others as persons are due just by virtue of having that capacity [apparently to any nonnull degree], so it should be given equally to all." But why should respect be thus equally parcelled out rather than, say, allotted (by a nonegalitarian application of the principle of distributive justice) in proportion to the degree to which persons possess the relevant empirical capacity invoked by Larmore? Any answer must appeal to some metaphysical, moral, or religious principles that form part of liberal comprehensive doctrines. I sketch what I take to be a plausible account of such principles in the last section of this chapter. But first, I say a bit more about liberal egalitarianism and empirical characteristics of persons.

But Aren't We, in Fact, All Equal?

It seems obvious that the simple answer to this question is "no." Regarding actual features ('occurrent' properties, in philosophers' jargon) of individuals falling within the species Homo sapiens, there is considerable diversity; and, insofar as we have access to what philosophers call 'dispositional' properties (capacities, abilities, aptitudes), there is reason to suppose—as we saw Larmore do with respect to the capacity for developing a coherent view of the world and of the good life—that many of these come in degrees that fall within a significantly wide range. If we wish to find equality, the way to do so is to abstract or prescind from the features with respect to which we are not equal. If we, in effect say, "let's discount all those respects in which we are not equal," we shall discover that we *are* equal in an analytic and fairly trivial way.

The question is why one should wish to interpret the empirical data in such a way as to obtain such egalitarian consequences? And the two most plausible types of answer are not surprising: (1) for pragmatic or prudential reasons; (2) for philosophical, moral, or religious commitments (namely, components of a comprehensive doctrine or conception of the good). I have suggested, with illustrations from Rawls and Larmore, that prudential or pragmatic considerations do not generally seem to be sufficient to obtain as general and as inclusive a form of egalitarian distributive justice as that to which liberalism is committed. That leaves answers of type (2): philosophical, moral, or religious commitments. Such commitments, in fact, structure political liberalism's (as well as perfectionist liberalism's) interpretation of what purport to be empirical data concerning human beings and their penchant for sociopolitical organization.

Quite characteristic of such an egalitarian interpretation of empirical data are Rawls's criteria for membership in what Vinit Haksar calls the "egalitarian club." Candidates are required to possess some powers, which would seem to come in degrees; and "[i]n having these powers to the essential minimum degree, citizens are equal."[26] For Rawls, these powers are

> a) the two moral powers, the capacity for a sense of justice and the capacity for a conception of the good. As necessary for the

exercise of the moral powers we add b) the intellectual powers of judgment, thought, and inference. Citizens are also assumed c) to have at any given time a determinate conception of the good interpreted in the light of a (reasonable) comprehensive view. Finally, we suppose d) that citizens have requisite capacities and abilities to be normal and cooperating members of society over a complete life.[27]

Haksar raises pertinent issues concerning such an approach to membership in the egalitarian club:

> It is sometimes said that all human beings should be given equal respect and consideration because they have equal intrinsic worth, but this shifts the problem. What are the grounds of equal human worth? . . . it is sometimes thought that human beings, unlike animals, have rationality. But some idiots are less rational than some animals, so why should we give more weight to the interests of idiots than to the interests of animals? Moreover, even among adult human beings some are more rational than others, so why should we not give greater intrinsic weight to the more rational ones? Similar problems arise with other suggested grounds for human equality, such as the capacity to form life-plans or ideals and follow them through with zest (William James), capacity for moral sentiments and for a sense of justice, self-consciousness, ability to use language, autonomy, and so forth. We could have a cut-off point which is high enough to exclude all non-human animals, but then there are problems about congenital idiots, and also other problems such as why those above the cut-off point should all get equal consideration. Even if there is nothing logically inconsistent about maintaining both that (a) those below the cut-off point (for instance, animals) should get lower status than those at or above the cut-off point, and that (b) those at or above the cut-off point should get equal weight in our moral calculations, one wants to know what is so sacred about the cut-off point? If the reason for giving creatures below that cut-off point lower worth is that they score less well on some test, then why not use similar tests to discriminate between those who are above the cut-off point.[28]

Haksar's own answer to these questions is complex. He holds that it is necessary to "postulate some kind of perfection-ist norm, for instance, that there is something rather wonder-ful about human beings who possess certain capacities (such as the capacity to lead a significant form of life) or the potential for them" (71). To obtain an egalitarian form of "equal respect," to form an egalitarian rather than hierarchical club, he is willing, however, to invoke pragmatic considerations, e.g., the conclusion that "[i]t is worth treating people equally even if they have unequal worth, because if we said that people with greater worth should get greater facilities, this will lead to considerable quarrels among individuals as to who are the superior ones," and the (skeptical) assertion that "[i]f differences of intrinsic worth between human beings were well-marked, then it would be feasible for political principles and policies to take such difference into account" but "in fact the differences are not well-marked" (69). Haksar is also willing to invoke pragmatic considerations for extending membership in the egalitarian club to some classes of human being that may, from the contemporary secular liberal perspective, seem at most borderline—e.g., congenital idiots, fetuses, the irreversibly comatose or terminally ill, neonates, infants and children. In sum, he envisions the possibility that "we can advance a perfectionist-cum-pragmatic presupposition of the doctrine of equality of respect and consideration between all human beings" (71).

Although Haksar believes that "perfectionist-cum-metaphysical considerations are presupposed by our egalitarian moral views" (81), he prefers a secular and 'sensible' metaphysical grounding—one that does not stray too far from the sorts of empirical properties and capacities that the application of current, secular common sense suggests might be relevant to membership in the liberal egalitarian club. The fact that he has recourse to pragmatic considerations to buttress his egalitarianism and smooth over certain problems will not please all liberals, as he recognizes. His discussion suggests that if one wishes to have a relatively simple, neat, and unproblematic account of membership in the liberal egalitarian club—if, in Haksar's words, "one wants to know what is so sacred about the cut-off point" with respect to the application of various empirical properties and capacities in determining membership in that club—then one's best bet is, in fact, to appeal literally or figuratively to the sacred. By "sacred", I mean some transempirical claim, originally deriving from a religious tradition, such as that we are all children of God, or that we all possess souls, or some secular surrogate for such a claim, such as that we all equally possess an inherent dignity due to our membership in the "kingdom of ends." Such transempirical bases of membership in the egalitarian club have what might be considered the disadvantage of not being firmly tied to obviously empirical properties or capacities. For example, Jeffrie G. Murphy has argued for a rather uncomfortable disjunction. Either (a) rationality, as a quasiempirical capacity, is not really coextensive with the supposedly equal human dignity or "worthiness of respect as a person" conferred by membership in the kingdom of ends or (b), if empirical rationality is coextensive with worthiness of respect, such "worthiness of respect as a person would seem to be a matter of *degree*—not something owed equally to all members of the human species." Consequently, "Kantianism, whatever Kant's actual intentions, seems to entail radical moral inegalitarianism."[29] There may indeed be epistemic liabilities resulting from separating at least to some degree such transempirical and egalitarian notions of sacredness, on the one hand, and properties and capacities that apparently are empirical, on the other. But effecting such a separation—"biting the bullet," religiously or metaphysically, in this matter—does have the advantage of attempting to prevent membership in the egalitarian club from being made more selective, on whatever grounds of expediency or current fashion that might be invoked. Such a consideration will have cogency only for those of us, liberals or not, who are concerned about such exclusions (e.g., fetuses, neonates, the comatose, mentally deficient persons, the terminally ill or very aged) and who may fear the presence of slippery slopes in this vicinity.

Liberalism's Best Bet?

In order to accord sufficient moral weight to membership in the egalitarian club and in order to make that club sufficiently inclusive and its boundaries sufficiently determinate, liberalism is probably best served by some transempirical notion of equal human sacredness, dignity, or worthiness of respect. But not just any such transempirical notion will serve liberalism's purposes. Christianity's notion of our common supernatural status as ensouled children of God is one transempirical notion of equal human worth that doubtless has exerted various egalitarian influences in Western sociopolitical cultures. But, as this

particular historical instance testifies, there are varieties of dignity, worth, and respect—even equal dignity, worth, and respect—that do not have the egalitarian consequences associated
with liberalism: e.g., equal possession of liberalism's particular civil and human freedoms, a notion of citizens who equally
share political authority, and (at least in the case of political
liberalism) the equal treatment of citizens supposedly manifested by the stance of political neutrality toward conceptions of
the good. According to a classical, not-necessarily-egalitarian,
conception of distributive justice, showing equal respect for
persons may require treating them very differently, e.g., pater-
nalistic treatment toward some but not others. As Ronald Dworkin rather paradoxically puts it, "[s]ometimes treating people
equally is the only way to treat them as equals; but sometimes
not."[30] In other words, in order to get the egalitarian consequences that liberalism wishes to obtain from a notion of human beings as equals with respect to fundamental, transempirical dignity, worth, or respect, liberalism requires a very special
notion of such equal dignity, worth, or respect. Christianity, for
most of its existence and in most of its forms, did not draw
such liberal egalitarian consequences from its conception of the
equal dignity or worthiness of respect of human beings. And it
would surely be facile to suppose that the only reasons Christianity did not draw such consequences were either (a) hypoc-
risy and bad faith or (b) a failure of rationality with respect to
its understanding of its own fundamental concepts.

The particular notion of equal dignity, worth, or respect that
works best for liberalism— liberalism's "best bet," as it were—
is a conception of citizens, members of the egalitarian club,
sharing equally in political authority. That is, each is to be
equally regarded as the author of at least the fundamental sociopolitical decisions of the society to which he or she belongs.
Historically, of course, such a notion of equal dignity found
especially clear expression in Rousseau's *Social Contract*:

> "How to find a form of association which will defend the per-
> son and goods of each member with the collective force of all,
> and under which each individual, while uniting himself with the
> others, obeys no one but himself, and remains as free as before."
> This is the fundamental problem to which the social contract holds
> the solution.[31]

Rousseau's answer to this "fundamental [and, indeed, huge] problem" is the abstract notion of the sovereign or general will:

> Now, as the sovereign is formed entirely of the individuals who compose it, it has not, nor could it have, any interest contrary to theirs; . . . The sovereign by the mere fact that it is, is always all that it ought to be.
> But this is not true of the relation of subject to sovereign. Despite their common interest, subjects will not be bound by their commitment unless means are found to guarantee their fidelity.
> For every individual as a man may have a private will contrary to, or different from, the general will that he has as a citizen. His private interest may speak with a very different voice from that of the public interest; . . .[32]

Decisions of the sovereign or general will (*la volonté générale*) are not necessarily to be equated with actual decisions of the government or the "will of all" (*la volonté de tous*: the majority of or even unanimous agreement of private wills). The general will, to be such, must express and be limited to those matters that could rationally be considered to be expressions of the interest of each and every citizen. As Rousseau puts it,

> [h]ow should it be that the general will is always rightful and that all men constantly wish the happiness of each but for the fact that there is no one who does not take that word "each" to pertain to himself and in voting think of himself? This proves that the equality of rights and the notion of justice which it produces derive from the predilection which each man has for himself and hence from human nature as such. It also proves that the general will, to be truly what it is, must be general in its purpose as well as in its nature; that it should spring from all and apply to all; and that it loses its natural rectitude when it is directed towards any particular and circumscribed object—for in judging what is foreign to us, we have no sound principle of equity to guide us.[33]

Rousseau's particular version of the 'bottom up' conception of sociopolitical authority explains a great deal about liberal egalitarianism. Its notion of practical rationality begins with *amour de soi-même*, i.e., natural self-regard, self-interest, or self-respect involving a notion of fairness that recognizes that other persons are similarly motivated and that this fact is a just limitation on the pursuit of self-interest. This limitation is what distinguishes virtuous *amour de soi-même* from vicious vanity, egoism, or greediness (*amour-propre*).[34] It is easy to move from such a conception of equal dignity to political liberalism's stance of neutrality with respect to conceptions of the good. According to a theory of equality endorsed by Ronald Dworkin,

> political decisions must be, so far as is possible, independent of any particular conception of the good life, or what gives value to life. Since citizens of a society differ in their conceptions, the government does not treat them as equals if it prefers one conception to another, either because the officials believe that one is intrinsically superior, or because one is held by the more numerous or powerful group.[35]

And, according to the Rousseauian conception of "treating as equals" or "acknowledging equal dignity and respect," the reason such a public privileging of one conception of good constitutes a breach of the duty of equal respect is that a citizen not sharing a particular conception of the good could not rationally be regarded as the author of a decision instantiating or derived from that conception (particularly if the decision in question is inconsistent with a conception of the good accepted by such a citizen). Indeed, at one point in *Political Liberalism*, Rawls uses such an argument:

> [C]itizens as free and equal have an equal share in the corporate political and coercive power of society, and all are equally subject to the burdens of judgment. There is no reason, then, why any citizen, or association of citizens, should have the right to use the state's police power to decide constitutional essentials or basic questions of justice as that person's, or that association's, comprehensive doctrine directs.[36]

The Rousseauian conception of equality of respect also nicely explains the liberal tradition's great emphasis on a notion of ideal rational justification or justifiability as the foundation of sociopolitical moral legitimacy. If the source of sociopolitical authority is the 'public' will of the person, the general will or the will of the person *qua citoyen*, then the legitimacy of sociopolitical decisions should be a function of what all persons, *qua citoyens*, would agree to. We cannot rely on what members of the sociopolitical community would *actually* agree to. For their actual decisions would doubtless often be manifestations of the *particularity* of their situations (including their particular conceptions of the good). From this liberal perspective, it is all too easy to equate any manifestation of particularity with uncooperative egoism—*amour-propre*. For it to be rational to regard "each" as equally the author of sociopolitical decisions, a particular notion of rational justification/justifiability is demanded: a notion that requires, at least with respect to fundamental sociopolitical decisions, that everyone "appropriate that word 'each' (*chacun*) to his own person."

Such a conception of 'public' practical rationality, the rationality of the *citoyen*, is the theoretical crystallization of liberalism's historiography of its own origins in concrete sociopolitical compromise. Of course, concrete political compromises and the modi vivendi to which they give rise are limited to certain specific issues and are by no means irrevocable. And the reasons and theoretical justification underlying such compromises will typically differ among the parties to them. But the liberal conception of justifiability demands an extension and idealization of this situation. Because each person must, morally, be considered an equal author of the society's fundamental sociopolitical decisions and, consequently, because each such decision must, morally, be justifiable to each person, the notion of justification involved must be entirely impersonal or 'public', in the terminology of the contemporary theory of political liberalism. That is, each such decision must be an expression of each individual's self-regard or *amour de soi-même*, where that *amour de soi-même* is entirely abstract and impersonal—i.e., the same from person to person.

Part of the force of a distinctively liberal conception of equal dignity, worth, or respect is captured by the Rousseauian conception of each party to a particular sociopolitical set-up as an equal author of its fundamental decisions. The common liberal emphasis on public or impersonal rational justifiability is a natural accompaniment to the Rousseauian conception. But practical rationality must have some first principles. If those principles are supplied by a notion of self-regard or *amour de soi-même*, equally distributed, what constitutes this liberal *amour de soi-même*? Here the liberal theorist has a choice, one that we have previously encountered, between (a) whatever, as a matter of contingent, empirical fact, citizens happen to have in common as constituents of their comprehensive conceptions of the good and (b) principles derived from some distinctive philosophical, moral, or religious doctrine, which will probably *not* be endorsed by all citizens.[37] Some liberal theorists (particularly those of perfectionist stripe) might want to add a third alternative: (c) principles respecting and furthering an inherent, equally shared personal autonomy, an autonomy interpreted as mandating the self-determination (usually within some moral boundaries) of comprehensive conceptions of the good. It is true that (c) is more general or inclusive—in the sense of permitting a wider, morally legitimate range of *determinate* conceptions of the good—than some traditional, pre-Enlightenment perfectionist doctrines falling under (b). But it seems clear that (c) is simply a special case of (b). That is, sustaining the sort of morally circumscribed autonomy postulated by (c) will ultimately appeal to philosophical, moral, or even religious assumptions of the same general type as those sustaining more determinate perfectionist doctrines. The fact that these assumptions, in the case of (c), may be compatible with or shared by a number of more determinate comprehensive conceptions does not mean that they cannot reasonably be denied or that there are not other respectable comprehensive doctrines that repudiate them.

Most liberal theorists, including contemporary theorists of political liberalism, have not been entirely comfortable with the first, pragmatic account (a) of the first principles of public, practical rationality. This account does not afford sufficient security to certain rights and principles that have come to be regarded as fundamental by many political liberals. For example, suppose that all members of a society, including those with a proclivity to homosexuality (if there is such a thing), were to agree that homosexual behavior violated their conceptions of the proper place of sexuality in human life. With the assumption of such agreement, every person could "appropriate that word 'each' to his own person" in voting to proscribe homosexual behavior. So would such a decision count as a legitimate expression of the general will? Each person could equally endorse or regard himself as the author of such a decision, because of the supposed empirical agreement among all persons' conceptions of the good (with respect to basic issues of sexuality). But would such a decision be a rational expression of the liberal conception of equal respect, worth, or dignity?

A great many late-twentieth-century liberals would agree with Dworkin that the answer is "no." The form of liberalism "based on equality," he claims,

> insists that government must treat people as equals in the following sense. It must impose no sacrifice or constraint on any citizen in virtue of an argument that the citizen could not accept without abandoning his sense of equal worth. This abstract principle requires liberals to oppose the moralism of the New Right, because no self-respecting person who believes that a particular way to live is most valuable for him can accept that this way of life is base or degrading. No self-respecting atheist can agree that a community in which religion is mandatory is for that reason finer, and no one who is homosexual that the eradication of homosexuality makes the community purer.[38]

When it comes to fleshing out the notion of recognizing the equal respect due to persons in a society, liberalism must appeal, at least implicitly, to some notion of the basis and implications of that equal respect and must address the question of what is equally worthy of respect in persons. A straightforward, empirical answer to this question is "whatever persons (at a given time and in a given society) agree in regarding as worthy of respect." But most liberal theorists are committed to stopping History, i.e., justifying and stabilizing a particular set of liberal freedoms and principles. If so, something beyond the vagaries of contingent empirical agreement is needed. And that "something beyond" is to be found in philosophical, moral, or religious presuppositions. The remarks by Dworkin concerning homosexuality can be made plausible by a group of such presuppositions, widely shared by late-twentieth-century liberals but by no means universally accepted, even in current Western society. (1) It is natural and appropriate for a person who possesses, for whatever reasons, homosexual proclivities to regard a homosexual life-style as a "particular way to live [that] is most valuable for him." (Frequent corollary: Any other attitude by the person with such proclivities is unnatural—the manifestation of socially induced neurosis—and not truly self-respecting.) (2) Choice among alternative sexual life-styles is a

freedom demanded by equal respect due persons because, most
plausibly, such a socially unconstrained choice and the working out of its consequences is regarded as central to the ideal
of Fulfilled Personhood, which is something like a personalized,
designer version of the old notion of human-nature-as-it-could-
be-if-it-realised-its-*telos*.

Presupposition (2), in turn, implies that there is much more
to sexuality, and indeed to finding one's niche within some
approved range of forms of sexual expression, than the obvious procreative function of sex and the fact that sexual activity, for most people, is a source of fairly intense if transient
physical pleasure. This implication, too, seems to have been
incorporated into one prominent version of the liberal position
with respect to sexual freedom and alternative expressions
of sexuality. In the words of Jeffrie Murphy, the dissenting
justices in the well-known U. S. Supreme Court sodomy case,
Bowers v. Hardwick, "suggested (whether rightly or wrongly)
that sexual freedom is special, a liberty worthy of special
protection as a fundamental right, because it often forms a part
of meaningful, virtuous, or—in short—good human lives."[39]
Murphy also suggests an analogy between the importance or
centrality of religious freedom and of sexual freedom, which is
manifest in the dissent to *Bowers v. Hardwick*. The dissenting
justices, he writes,

> seemed to see sexual freedom as analogous to religious free-
> dom in at least this way: it often forms a part of the very fabric
> of meaning and worth in an individual life. Often it is not sim-
> ply a recreational amusement [and, as Murphy might have added
> but did not, "not simply a means for procuring children"] but is
> rather a part of what is involved in participating in those rela-
> tionships that are among the crowning glories of human exist-
> ence—relationships of love and personal intimacy.[40]

The placing of sex, as such, in such an exalted position—
and certainly the extension of this attitude toward forms
of sexual expression beyond heterosexual matrimony—is indic-
ative of the influence of the so-called sexual revolution on liberal theory. If the attitudes associated with the sexual revolution
do represent a developing—although by no means complete—
consensus in Western constitutional democracies, we have some

further evidence that theorists of political liberalism are not entirely misguided in seeing actual sociopolitical compromise and consensus as being so central to both the conceptual core and the historiography of liberalism. But to stop History, to justify and to stabilize the results of such compromise, theory is needed. Murphy and many other contemporary philosophers and sociopolitical theorists are correct in seeing such theory as ultimately resting on perfectionist foundations.[41]

The preceding discussion suggests that liberalism's "best bet" is a complicated matter. To begin with, the Rousseauian version of equality of respect, dignity, or worth requires that each person be able rationally to regard himself or herself as the author of each decision, at least with respect to the fundamentals, of the sociopolitical order to which he or she belongs. This version of equality of respect appears nicely to accommodate liberal neutrality: for each person to be able to regard himself or herself as the author of each fundamental decision, such decisions must not issue from particular comprehensive conceptions of the good not shared throughout the community. It also nicely explains the emphasis, within much of contemporary theory of political liberalism, on 'public' justifiability. Finally, this version provides an answer to the question constituting the title of this chapter: "What Ever Happened to Distributive Justice?" Answer: It has not disappeared from the liberal tradition but has assumed the following egalitarian form. Because we all are equal with respect to sharing in the authority of the state, we should (a), in some way, share equally in the political decision-making process and (b), in some sense, share equally in the burdens and benefits resulting from sociopolitical cooperation.

However, in order to stop History (to justify, legitimate, stabilize, and entrench liberal consensus), liberalism must appeal to some assumptions about what is worthy of equal political respect among persons constituting a particular political society. I do not lay any claim to originality in suggesting that this appeal will ultimately rest on some philosophical, moral, or religious—and perfectionist—components of comprehensive conceptions of the human good. For such a project of justification to be safe from empirical vicissitudes, a transempirical foundation of equality of respect has its advantages. What, precisely, is included in the liberal agenda, and what is deemed worthy of being accorded equal respect and protection, will determine the content of a particular variety of liberalism's notion of Fulfilled Personhood. In general, however, the content of Fulfilled Personhood will refer to those areas of life that (1) are deemed Pretty Important (or, in Haksar's memorable phrase, "rather wonderful") and (2) are assumed ideally to be subject to self-determination or self-development. Many of liberalism's freedoms, classical and not-so-classical (e.g., religious freedom and sexual freedom, respectively), would seem to be most plausibly justified by the assumptions that (a) the behavior to which they pertain is central to the notion of Fulfilled Personhood, (b) there is a range of morally permissible choices to be made with respect to such behavior, and (c) a considerable part of the very value of such behavior, vis-à-vis Fulfilled Personhood, is the unconstrained (and rational?)[42] making of such choices and the consequent living out of one's life in conformity with those choices.

Assumptions of this sort certainly seem to involve judgments about the human good. To consider the example of liberal religious freedom, an underlying assumption seems to be that religiosity in general—within some limited range of morally permissible expression—can but need not be closely tied to the notion of Fulfilled Personhood. Such a liberal conception of religious freedom presupposes, to begin with, the possibility of an independent moral stance from which what is morally acceptable in religion and what is not may be determined. This assumption has often been denied in Western philosophical and religious thought. The liberal conception also seems to presuppose that what is important, at least for some persons, is the development of the "religious impulse" (within a certain set of constraints). But this, too, is surely a controversial assumption. An alternative, traditional view, further discussed in chapter 4, which has been and continues to be appealing to many religious persons, is that religiosity *qua* religiosity is of, at most, derivative value. In its most erroneous forms, religion is the cause of great mischief. Consequently, if one is not going to get it basically right with respect to religion, it would perhaps be better to eschew this supposed religious impulse altogether.

So, should contemporary liberal theorists give up the distinctive stance of political liberalism with respect to neutrality and embrace some form of perfectionist liberalism? This move is not without its appeal. It even would be possible to retain many of the consequences of the stance of neutrality. The justification of these consequences would come not from the supposed value of the stance of neutrality as such, but rather from the value, for the development of Fulfilled Personhood, of the liberty of self-determination—within some limits and with respect to select kinds of behavior.

The price to be paid for the move to forthright perfectionism, however, is substantial: the cutting loose of liberalism from its historiographical moorings. Contemporary political liberalism, as we saw in the first chapter, tends to see itself as a theoretical expression of post-Reformation, Enlightenment compromise and consensus—*the* distinctive sociopolitical theory of moderation, toleration, and sweet reasonableness. One result, previously mentioned, is the tendency of liberalism to regard itself as having uniquely staked out the moral high ground in the sociopolitical debate. Another result, also previously mentioned, is liberalism's desire to stop History by developing a theory intended to justify, morally, a set of liberal institutions, practices, and principles; such a theory is also supposed to have the practical effect of stabilizing those liberal institutions, practices, and principles.

To adopt forthright perfectionism would be to relinquish the special and privileged position that many proponents see liberalism as occupying with respect to sociopolitical theory. In some ways, such a move would be analogous to the disestablishment of a national church, which can then no longer regard itself as the particular guardian of the nation's morality and spirituality nor regard itself (in the way that the Church of England has often regarded itself) as the ecclesial embodiment of a national religious consensus or modus vivendi. The theoretical disestablishment of liberalism, then, would entail its joining the theoretical fray. But this move points up the importance of reexamining political liberalism's conception of what it has taken to be its distinctive mission. In the next chapter, I consider various aspects of political liberalism's conception of this mission.

Notes

1. Aristotle, *Ethica Nicomachea*, ed. I. Bywater (Oxford: Clarendon Press, 1962), 5.2.1130b31–33.
2. Ibid., 5.3.1131a25–29.
3. Plato, *Republica*, ed. J. Burnet (Oxford: Clarendon Press, 1965), 4.433a5–6 and 433e11–12.
4. St. Thomas Aquinas, *Summa Theologiae*, ed. P. Caramello (Turin and Rome: Marietti, 1952), II^a II^{ae}, q. 58, a. 11.
5. Bernard Häring, C.SS.R., *The Law of Christ*, trans. Edwin G. Kaiser, C.PP.S., vol. 1 (Westminster, Md.: The Newman Press, 1961), 520–21. I shall cite the English translation of Häring's *Das Gesetz Christi* (*The Law of Christ*) for accurate and lucid (if occasionally somewhat verbose) presentation of Roman Catholic moral teaching. Subsequent to the appearance of this work, after the Second Vatican Council, Häring gained notoriety as a heterodox dissenter from many of the doctrines he had previously vigorously upheld. Consequently, there should be no presumption that the doctrine of *Das Gesetz* represents his subsequent (or current) views.
6. Jacques Maritain, *The Rights of Man and Natural Law*, trans. Doris C. Anson (New York: Charles Scribner's Sons, 1943), 36.
7. Ibid. "To sum up, the fundamental rights, like the right to existence and life: the right to personal freedom or to conduct one's own life as master of oneself and of one's acts, responsible for them before God and the law of the community; the right to the pursuit of the perfection of moral and rational human life; the right to the pursuit of eternal good (without this pursuit there is no true pursuit of happiness); the right to keep one's body whole; the right to private ownership of material goods, which is a safeguard of the liberties of the individual; the right to marry according to one's choice and to raise a family which will be assured of the liberties due it; the right of association, the respect for human dignity in each individual, whether or not he represents and economic value for society—all these rights are rooted in the vocation of the person (a spiritual and free agent) to the order of absolute values and to a destiny superior to time. The French Declaration of the Rights of Man framed these rights in the altogether rationalist point of view of the Enlightenment and the Encyclopedists, and to that extent developed them in ambiguity. The American Declaration of Independence, however marked by the influence of Locke and 'natural religion', adhered more closely to the originally Christian character of human rights" (79–80).
8. Michael Walzer, *Thick and Thin: Moral Argument at Home and Abroad* (Notre Dame, Ind.: University of Notre Dame Press, 1994), 21.
9. Aristotle, *Ethica Nicomachea* 5.2.1131a1.
10. Thomas Hobbes, *De cive*, bk. 2, chap. 6, trans. Thomas Hobbes,

in *Man and Citizen*, ed. Bernard Gert (Garden City, N. Y.: Anchor Books, 1972), 139–140.

11. Ibid., bk. 4, chap. 9, 178.

12. Hobbes, *Leviathan: Parts I and II*, ed. Herbert Schneider (Indianapolis, Ind.: The Bobbs-Merrill Company, Inc. 1958), pt. 1, chap. 15, 127.

13. Hobbes, *De cive*, bk. 1, chap. 3, 114.

14. Hobbes, *Leviathan*, pt. 1, chap. 13, 107.

15. John Locke, *Second Treatise of Government*, ed. C. B. Macpherson (Indianapolis, Ind.: Hackett Publishing Company, Inc., 1980), chap. 5, sec. 26, 18.

16. C. B. Macpherson, editor's introduction to John Locke, *Second Treatise of Government*, xxi.

17. John Rawls, *Political Liberalism*, 262.

18. Richard Hooker, *Of the Laws of Ecclesiastical Polity*, bk. 1, quoted in John Locke, *Second Treatise of Government*, chap. 2, sec. 5, 8–9.

19. Locke, *Second Treatise of Government*, chap. 2, sec. 4.

20. Ibid., sec. 6.

21. Rawls, *Political Liberalism*, 63.

22. Ibid., 54.

23. Jean-Jacques Rousseau, *The Social Contract*, trans. Maurice Cranston (New York: Penguin Books, 1968), bk. 2 , chap. 4, 75.

24. Rawls, *Political Liberalism*, 5–6.

25. Charles Larmore, *Patterns of Moral Complexity* (Cambridge: Cambridge University Press, 1987), 59.

26. Rawls, *Political Liberalism*, 81.

27. Ibid.

28. Vinit Haksar, *Equality, Liberty, and Perfectionism* (Oxford: Oxford University Press, 1979), 18–19.

29. Jeffrie G. Murphy, "Afterword: Constitutionalism, Moral Skepticism, and Religious Belief," in *Constitutionalism: The Philosophical Dimension*, Contributions in Legal Studies, no. 46, ed. Alan S. Rosenbaum (New York: Greenwood Press, 1988), 245.

30. Ronald Dworkin, "Liberalism," in *A Matter of Principle* (Cambridge, Mass.: Harvard University Press, 1985), 190.

31. Rousseau, *The Social Contract*, bk. 1, chap. 6, 60.

32. Ibid., chap. 7, 63.

33. Ibid., bk. 2, chap. 4, 75.

34. For the distinction between *amour de soi-même* and *amour-propre*, see Rousseau's *Discours sur l'inégalité*, especially note *o* in the Vaughan edition: *The Political Writings of Jean-Jacques Rousseau*, ed. C. E. Vaughan, vol. 1 (New York: John Wiley and Sons, Inc., 1962), 217.

35. Dworkin, "Liberalism," 191.

36. Rawls, *Political Liberalism*, 61–62.

37. Rawls appeals to his concept of "primary goods" here: "[n]ow

the assumption is that though men's rational plans do have different final ends, they nevertheless all require for their execution certain primary goods, natural and social. Plans differ since individual abilities, circumstances, and wants differ; rational plans are adjusted to these contingencies. But whatever one's system of ends, primary goods are necessary means" (John Rawls, *A Theory of Justice* [Cambridge, Mass.: The Belknap Press, 1971], 93). Rawls's notion of primary goods, particularly the "primary social goods," represents not so much an empirical claim about the consilience of human wants and needs as a theory about what certain rational agents, curtained behind the veil of ignorance and thus ignorant of the determinate content of their comprehensive conceptions of the good, would choose by way of means for achieving such (indeterminate) ends. In this way, he claims to obtain a set of common liberal "rights and liberties" as primary social goods. As a number of commentators have argued, this result certainly appears to favor some comprehensive doctrines or conceptions of the good over others and, thus, is not really neutral in its import.

38. Dworkin, "Why Liberals Should Care about Equality," in *A Matter of Principle*, 205–206.

39. Jeffrie G. Murphy, "Legal Moralism and Liberalism," *Arizona Law Review* 37, no. 1 (Spring, 1995): 86.

40. Ibid.

41. See also J. G. Murphy, "Kant on Theory and Practice," in *Theory and Practice*, ed. Ian Shapiro and Judith Wagner DeCew (New York: New York University Press, 1995), 65: "And what about sexual freedom— e.g., for homosexuals? We surely cannot even begin to make a case for such freedom as fundamental without developing an account of love, sexuality, intimacy, and the role they play in a full and good human life. If we see sexual freedom purely as freedom of recreational pleasure, we will trivialize it and make it a very poor candidate indeed for a fundamental liberty. Could we imagine all citizens reasonably consenting to repressive rules with respect to homosexuality? If sex is just recreation, I think the answer is yes. If sex is more deeply tied to the good life, however, I think the answer is no."

42. The Kantian strain within liberalism puts particular emphasis on the term "rational" in the phrase "rational autonomy," where rational autonomy is taken to be constitutive of Fulfilled Personhood. As a number of philosophers, including my colleague Jeff Murphy, have argued, it is far from obvious how such a notion could be invoked in support of various external freedoms now deemed important in liberal theory. Is, for example, the freedom to buy (and sell and distribute) pornography somehow necessary to or an essential expression of one's Kantian, inner rational autonomy? John Finnis, for example, apparently thinks not. For Kant, he claims, "the duty to treat oneself as an end, as honor-

able, and not merely as means to gratifying one's own or others' inclinations, is a duty which can only be truly and fully fulfilled by maintaining a certain intention/disposition (*Gesinnung*)" (J. M. Finnis, "Legal Enforcement of 'Duties to Oneself': Kant v. Neo-Kantians," *Columbia Law Review* 87, no. 3 [April, 1987]: 451–52.).

Chapter 3

Stopping History—By the Rules

I have used the phrase "to stop History" for that part of the program of political liberalism pertaining to the moral justification and stabilization of what liberalism regards as the results of sociopolitical compromise and consensus. It might be claimed that any sociopolitical theory worthy of the name would want thus to justify its recommendations and, if possible, entrench their institutional realization. However, liberalism is almost unique among such theories in seeing its desiderata, in the sociopolitical sphere, as the product of natural social, political, and economic forces while, at the same time, committing itself to justifying the moral correctness and entrenching the institutionalization of those desiderata. Hence the phrase "to stop History": to justify and legitimate, to stabilize and entrench the results of certain sociopolitical compromises arising from the particular and apparently contingent social developments within post-Reformation and Enlightenment northern Europe. Of course, most contemporary theorists of political liberalism will focus on certain features of actual historical compromise as worthy of justification and entrenchment. They typically will see actual historical developments, even in contemporary liberal constitutional democracies, as only approximating some theoretical ideal. But many liberal theorists will see such an ideal, however far removed it may be from actual, grimy political practice, as somehow implicit in the sociopolitical developments constituting the historical background of contemporary liberalism—or in the product of those developments (e.g., Rawls's "political culture of a democratic society").

I have just claimed that liberalism is "almost unique" in seeking to justify and entrench the contingent result of historical development and, in this sense, to stop History at a certain sociopolitical juncture. Orthodox, nonutopian Marxist socialism doubtless sees the stopping of History (at History's End, *beyond* anything that liberalism has wrought) as a Good Thing. However, the conflation of the normative and the factual in 'scientific' Marxism's deterministic conception of historical development means, in effect, that History stops Itself—and where else but at Its End? In chapter 1, I suggested that perhaps many contemporary liberal theorists would like to think that the basic principles, practices, and institutions of liberalism—in some perfected, polished up, and lacquered form—represent a natural terminus in the development of sociopolitical organization. Apart from the decidedly minority Hegel-Kojève-Fukuyama tradition, however, few liberal theorists have had the temerity to suggest that History will be so accommodating as to stop where they would like It to stop. Hence, the need to stop It by means of the construction of a justifying and entrenching theory. Herbert Marcuse writes that the sociopolitical positivism of Comte and the "original philosophies of counter-revolution sponsored by Bonald and De Maistre were committed to the repudiation of man's claim to alter and reorganize his social institutions in accordance with his rational will."[1] Much of contemporary political liberalism is committed to the affirmation of the claim, not so much to "alter and reorganize," but to justify and preserve liberal social principles, attitudes, and institutions "in accordance with [the *citoyen's*] rational will."[2]

What I referred to at the conclusion of the preceding chapter as political liberalism's distinctive mission is to stop History by means of theory—to construct a theory that will serve the dual functions of (a) morally justifying and legitimating and (b) stabilizing and entrenching some purified and perfected extrapolation from the political compromises that, according to liberalism's own favored historiography, constitute its post-Reformation and Enlightenment historical roots. However, in fulfilling its mission of stopping History, political liberalism sets significant constraints for itself: it must play by the rules of the game. Political liberalism must address several related questions in the course of attending to its mission. Exactly what and how much of historical post-Reformation, Enlightenment socio-political compromise is to be justified and entrenched? And why that particular bit? Two questions seem to be unavoidable: What rules for the justifying and entrenching game are to be adopted? What part of the content of actual political compromise and consensus is to be justified and entrenched? The conceptual content and history of liberalism provide some indication of what the answers to these questions should be. I argue, however, that the result of following up on these "indications" places severe strain on the conceptual fabric of political liberalism. Liberalism, of course, has a history of its own—one that has now been continuously augmented over the last three or four centuries. As is the case with many other concepts, its history has provided liberalism not only with theoretical development and conceptual richness but also with problems—tensions, ambiguities, and vacillations that threaten the logical coherence of the liberal enterprise. Signs of such problems are to be found in contemporary political liberalism.

To Justify or To Stabilize?

An assumption of much of contemporary political theory that might be characterized by the label "political liberalism" was mentioned toward the end of chapter 1. The preeminent function of political theory is to provide the theoretical means whereby (1) some set of liberal principles, attitudes, and institutions may be justified or legitimated in some moral or normative manner and (2) these principles, attitudes, and institutions may thereby be stabilized and entrenched. The "thereby" is both significant and problematic. The term "stability" suggests an empirical social phenomenon that surely might be of considerable pragmatic political importance. By "empirical social phenomenon" I do not necessarily mean something that is straightforwardly and uncontroversially observable. The Soviet sociopolitical system seemed to me, as a cold-war child of the 'fifties and early 'sixties, quite stable. But hindsight now makes that judgment seem mistaken. One can imagine a social scientist devising a sociopolitical stability index—and perhaps it has in fact been done. But it is likely that any such instrument would prove controversial and highly defeasible. What seems quite bizarre is that theorists of political liberalism would assume that *theoretical* justification of liberal attitudes, practices, and institutions should have any very strong positive correlation with the empirical stability of those attitudes, practices, and institutions.

Is the apparent assumption of such correlation simply a manifestation of political theoreticians' (or philosophers') hubris? The matter is considerably more complex, and interesting, than that. The very conceptual structure of liberalism, along with its own favored historiography, lead to a distinctive conflation of the empirical and the theoretical with respect to issues of 'stability'. According to a quite reasonable reading of Rawls's *A Theory of Justice* by Thomas E. Hill, Jr., one of the tasks of political philosophy is to "offer considerations for believing that a society well ordered by those principles of justice [scil., derived from a particular theory of justice] would be stable."[3] This appears to be an issue concerning stability in a fairly straightforward, empirical sense of the term. Note, however, that the issue seems to be raised as an additional consideration for political philosophy. That is, it seems to be a matter of developing a political theory of justice and then considering the important but subsidiary question of whether such principles of justice would be supportive of or conducive to social stability. As Hill makes clear, another preliminary task of political theory is presupposed: "justifying fundamental principles of justice regarding the basic political and economic institutions."[4] So it appears that such a theory of justice is not to be justified exclusively or primarily by the fact that is supportive of or conducive to social stability—because, e.g., the theory of justice in question is actually endorsed by the consensus of citizens.

When we turn to Rawls's *Political Liberalism*, it becomes clear that he is minimally concerned with what he terms "stability as a purely practical matter":

> Perhaps we think there are two separate tasks: one is to work out a political conception that seems sound, or reasonable, at least to us; the other is to find ways to bring others who reject it also to share it; or failing that, to act in accordance with it, if need be prompted by state power. As long as the means of persuasion or enforcement can be found, the conception is viewed as stable.

But, as a liberal conception, justice as fairness is concerned with stability in a different way. Finding a stable conception is not simply a matter of avoiding futility. Rather, what counts is the kind of stability, the nature of the forces that secure it.[5]

"The kind of stability," Rawls concludes, "[that is] required of justice as fairness is based, then, on its being a liberal political view, one that aims at being acceptable to citizens as reasonable and rational, as well as free and equal, and so as addressed to their public reason."[6] In other words, the "stability" that is of concern to Rawls is not an empirical matter secured by actual compromise, consensus, or modus vivendi. Indeed, he maintains that his notion of a "political conception of justice" "is not political in the wrong way: that is, its form and content are not affected by the existing balance of political power between comprehensive doctrines."[7] Rawlsian "stability" is an essentially moral and theoretical matter. It is a matter of what citizens who are "rational and reasonable" as well as "free and equal" (autonomous, self-interested, symmetrically situated) *should* be able to agree to when they utilize only their "public reason."

The moral theory at work here seems to be essentially the Rousseauian one discussed in the preceding chapter: "stable" is what idealized, practically rational and symmetrically situated agents could (should) agree to in situations where it would be "rational and reasonable" for everyone to "appropriate that word 'each' (*chacun*) to his own person." The combination of rationality and reasonableness as expressed in citizens' public reason (discussed later in this chapter) amounts to the rational expression of Rousseau's *amour de soi-même*. No more for Rawls than for Rousseau is the political conception of justice, also known as the general will, to be equated with "the will of all." And, consequently, the stability that is of primary interest to Rawls depends only on the consent of the rational and the reasonable in situations where each can rationally identify himself or herself with all.

But what, then, does this Rawlsian stability have to do with the real (empirical) item? This question exercises two commentators on Rawls's recent contributions to political liberalism. In presenting his initial reading of Rawls's attempt in *Political Liberalism* to address the stability problem, Thomas Hill suggests

that Rawls's new solution "seems to be not to reject or dramatically revise the content of justice as fairness [as presented
in Rawls's *A Theory of Justice*] but to reconceive it and present
it in a new light."[8] This new light turns out to be the supposed
tertium quid, to which I alluded in chapter 1: something between, in Hill's words, "*uniformity* of doctrine" and a "mere
modus vivendi among adherents of different doctrines" (339).
The content of the supposed *tertium quid* is a freestanding
political and liberal conception of justice, which reasonable
and rational citizens should be able to agree to irrespective of
their comprehensive doctrines (as long as those doctrines are
rational and reasonable). Because such a liberal political conception of justice is supposed to fit as a sort of detachable
module in rational and reasonable comprehensive doctrines, it
can procure stability by winning the assent of an "overlapping
consensus of reasonable doctrines." And, as Hill notes,

> stability based in this way on an overlapping consensus of doc-
> trines is supposed to be enhanced by the idea of *public reason*: that
> is, the idea that we are (voluntarily) to restrict our arguments [in
> the public sphere], on matters affecting the basic structure of soci-
> ety, to political arguments drawn from within the limits of com-
> mon reason and our working political conception of justice. In
> other words, barring emergencies, we are not to appeal to our
> particular comprehensive religious and philosophical doctrines in
> public debates about the most fundamental political institutions.
> Such restraint should reduce divisiveness on the basic political
> institutions and so contribute further to stability (339).

Hill suggests—quite rightly—that "if we see the main point
of *Political Liberalism* as an attempt to assuage the practical
concern about stability, then its arguments, I suspect, are bound
to seem woefully inadequate" (341). Depending on how restric-
tive Rawls's notion of a rational and reasonable comprehensive
doctrine turns out to be—an issue to which I shall return—it
might turn out that such liberal doctrines are held by something considerably less than an overwhelming majority of citizens. Rawlsian stability, then, has nothing to say about citizens
whose comprehensive doctrines are not gathered under the liberal umbrella of rationality and reasonableness and, to that
extent, does not represent a "practical concern about stability."
Hill also has some doubts that are akin to my earlier worries

about justifying the less controversial by the more controversial and concerning the role of theory in producing "stability as a practical concern":

> Fortunately, we have somehow developed in the United States a considerable consensus on our constitution and associated political procedures, but when we raise questions of interpretation and philosophical justification the consensus seems to evaporate . . . The core tenets of political liberalism, I suppose, are more readily understood and accepted than the fully specified versions (such as justice as fairness), but I suspect that the same forces that generate divergence of moral and religious comprehensive doctrines will block consensus on the less comprehensive, but still philosophical, political ideas of liberalism.
>
> Moreover, the arguments of *Political Liberalism*, seem quite inadequate, and of the wrong kind, to solve the stability problem as I have presented it. What makes for stability in a society is largely an empirical question; and *Political Liberalism* does not purport to offer empirical evidence that an overlapping consensus would be likely. . . .
>
> Again, if a practical concern for durability and stabilizing forces is the focus of concern, then *Political Liberalism* seems to rely too heavily on appeals to rational judgment. The factors which stabilize various societies may in fact have relatively little to do with the systems of ideas that they espouse, and more to do with habit, reinforcement, and blind emotional attachments. These factors may also be highly contextual, and so not transferable from one historical situation to another (341–42)

Hill concludes that Rawls is not much concerned in *Political Liberalism* with stability as a practical matter but with the issue of the moral legitimacy of political institutions. Rawls's primary aim

> is to give a defense of justice as fairness against the charge that (even if we had power to do so) to use it as a standard for (inevitably) coercive political decisions would violate the liberal principle of legitimacy. That principle says, "our exercise of political power is fully proper only when it is exercised in accordance with a constitution of essentials of which all citizens as free and equal may reasonably be expected to endorse in the light of principles and ideals acceptable to their common human reason" (346).

While Hill seems to be not entirely uncomfortable with this result, the same is not true for Brian Barry. In *Political Liberal-*

ism, Rawls suggests that his liberal account of "justice as fairness is best presented in two stages. In the first stage it is worked out as freestanding political (but of course moral) conception for the basic structure of society."[9] The second stage involves an examination of its Rawlsian stability, in the rather Pickwickian sense of this term we have just been considering: The conception of justice will be "stable" just in case it can be endorsed by those liberal rational and reasonable comprehensive doctrines into which it can be fitted as a module. Barry, in effect, makes the point that it is not very surprising that Rawls's political conception of justice as fairness proves to be stable in this sense: This interpretation

> recruits to the "overlapping consensus" only those for whom membership is irrelevant to stability. For the mechanism can operate only on those who already accept the principles of justice in virtue of their derivation within the "political conception." And these people, as Rawls says, already have the Scanlonian motivation for respecting the demands of justice [i.e., the desire to act according to rules that could not reasonably be rejected by others similarly motivated].[10]

Barry is saying that Rawls's "second stage," with which he is preoccupied in *Political Liberalism*, is otiose. Rawlsian stability apparently has little to do with actual, empirical social stability (Hill's stability "as a practical concern"). And, in Barry's opinion, what Rawlsian "stability" *is* concerned with— the moral legitimacy of institutions enshrining his principles of justice—is more adequately and less ambiguously addressed in the "first stage," the working out of the principles of justice "as a freestanding (but of course moral) conception." *In practice*, Barry suggests, Rawls's discussion of the "second stage" in *Political Liberalism* seems to have resulted in diminished commitment to the economic egalitarianism of Rawls's second principle of justice, the "difference principle," according to which socioeconomic inequalities are just only if they stand to benefit the least advantaged members of society. It is to be doubted, as Rawls himself perhaps suggests,[11] that all comprehensive doctrines that are rational and reasonable (in Rawls's sense, whatever precisely that is) could endorse this principle. According to Barry, in writings subsequent to *Political Liberalism*, Rawls appears to suggest that a first-stage "political derivation" of liberal principles of justice "need not incorporate the egalitarian commitment" in the socioeconomic sphere built into the difference principle. Barry comments that "[t]his is, it seems to me, no more than a logical working out of the conditions of stability as Rawls now conceives them. If the second principle [of justice, the difference principle] cannot be sustained at the second stage, it must be excised from the first stage too."[12]

My intention in this discussion has not been to engage in exegesis of Rawls (or of commentators on Rawls) for its own sake. Rather it has been to illustrate what seems to me to be a striking phenomenon: the lack of a clear distinction, at least within the Rawlsian tradition of political liberalism, between the *empirical* issue of social stability, on the one hand, and the issue of the *moral legitimacy* of sociopolitical principles and institutions, on the other. This does not seem to be a particularly subtle or difficult distinction to make; and the theorists of political liberalism I have been discussing, Rawls, Hill, and Barry, certainly seem to be perfectly aware of its existence. Why, then, the conflation? I suggest that the combination of liberalism's historiography and its conceptual commitments makes the conflation a very natural, if not altogether unavoidable, consequence. On the one hand, there is liberalism's historical provenance, according to its own favored historiography, in actual, concrete compromise and consensus, i.e., various post-Reformation and Enlightenment modi vivendi. Here the empirical stability of such compromises and the modi vivendi to which they give rise is a matter of the actual continuing agreement of most of the participants, for whatever reasons or causes and on whatever terms. And, surely, the political legitimacy of such concrete, piecemeal compromises and *modi vivendi* would seem largely to be a matter of consensus and acquiescence—what the parties are actually willing to agree to or are willing tacitly to accept.

But when liberalism, including political liberalism, sets out to stop History by means of theory—that is, to justify or legitimate a *particular* set of liberal principles, institutions, and attitudes—it typically assumes that it needs something more than the contingent, limited, and revocable results of piecemeal sociopolitical compromise. I have suggested that the most plau-

sible candidate for the "something more" is an idealized notion of consensus, a Rousseauian general will, consisting of justifiability to symmetrically situated citizens and appealing only
to their rational and reasonable *amour de soi-même*. The more a
liberal theory, such as Rawls's, concentrates on this enterprise
of justification or legitimation, the less relevant will be what
citizens actually agree to, which, as Hill points out, "may in
fact have relatively little to do with the systems of ideas they
espouse"[13] Nor will what citizens actually agree to or acqui-
esce in have much to do with the highly idealized—not to say
loaded—notion of practical rationality and reasonableness that
is generally required by liberal theorists in order to obtain the
results that they desire from their justifying theory. To obtain
justification from their invocation of the Rousseauian model
for some determinate set of liberal freedoms and principles,
liberal theorists need some determinate constraints on a
constellation of notions: rationality, reasonableness, public
reason—and the notion of Fulfilled Personhood (the object of
amour de soi-même) that is supposed to be furthered by the liberal polity that results from the successful exercise of public,
practical rationality and reasonableness.

Liberal justification/legitimation theory, on this account,
becomes a sort of "ideal observer" or "ideal agent" theory. The
real conceptual import of such theories is typically determined
by the specifics that are assumed concerning the "ideal" situation. That is, the whole mechanism of the ideal observers/agents
themselves, what they would say or agree to, becomes nonessential window dressing.[14] Barry's complaint about the otiosity
of Rawls's "second stage" in presenting his theory of justice
is a consequence of this fact. The real work is done at the
first stage, in the derivation of the principles of justice in conformity with the dictates of the political use of rationality and
reasonableness in a suitably idealized context of symmetrically
situated, self-interested agents. The supposed "second stage,"
which addresses the issue of Rawlsian stability (i.e., the justifiability of the results of the first stage to citizens holding reasonable comprehensive doctrines), does not really add anything
substantive to the enterprise of the first stage—and has the
potential for being misunderstood.

Political liberalism's mission of stopping History by the theoretical legitimation of a particular set of liberal principles, institutions, and attitudes has the effect of diminishing the concern of liberal theorists with the empirical stability that is intimately connected with what people are actually willing to agree to, or at least what they are willing to put up with. But political liberalism's historiographical conception of its own origins in concrete agreements has generally made its theorists loath to divorce altogether its mission of legitimation from such considerations. Hence the concern within the liberal tradition with *actual* consensus, with such notions as "consent of the governed" and "democratic representation." Indeed, a common observation within the liberal tradition is the tension, perhaps particularly manifest in contemporary political liberalism, between the mission of stopping History by developing a theoretical legitimation of a particular, determinate set of liberal principles, institutions, and attitudes and maintaining a sensitivity to the historical liberal commitment to the "will of the people" (Rousseau's *la volonté de tous*, as opposed to his *la volonté générale*), as expressed in various concrete agreements and modi vivendi. Not surprisingly, a common focus of liberalism's often implicit attempt to deal with this tension is some ideal of practical rationality peculiar to the public or political realm.

"Come now, and let us reason together, saith the Lord" (Is. 1:18)

This quotation from the prophet Isaias supposedly was the favorite verse in the Bible of that sometime practicing liberal and former U.S. president Lyndon Baines Johnson. He no doubt often invoked it (tactfully omitting the "saith the Lord") in the midst of the log-rolling, button-holing, and arm-twisting he employed to effect that amazing (but short-lived) congressional consensus and modus vivendi to which he applied such phrases as "War on Poverty" and "Great Society." As it happens (and as Johnson was probably fully aware), the quotation is quite apt because the context makes it clear that the Lord was involved in some carrot-and-stick negotiations with Israel. When we turn to the role of reasonableness, rationality, public and political reason in the theory of contemporary political

liberalism, it is salutary to remember Isaias and LBJ as illustrations of what the appeal to be reasonable and to reason together can amount to in concrete sociopolitical situations.

Of course, the notions of public reason typically invoked by
contemporary theories of political liberalism are rather more
exalted and also of central importance. Several important theoretical variants of political liberalism hope to find here that
elusive *tertium quid*: a foundation of liberal principle, institutions, and attitudes that does not depend on either (1) the
nonjustification of simply resting content with whatever the
rough-and-tumble of concrete political compromise yields in
particular issues or (2) the appeal to a particular religious,
philosophical, or moral doctrine (i.e., Rawlsian comprehensive
conception of the good). The hope is that an appropriate
conception of practical, public rationality and reasonableness may help supply the means for avoiding what most
contemporary theorists of political liberalism regard as these
unpalatable extremes.

But why are the extremes unpalatable? Why isn't one or the
other of these obvious alternatives good enough? With respect
to (1), liberalism has not been willing completely to abandon
actual agreement, no matter how it is obtained and on what
grounds it is accepted (short of manifest coercion), as playing
a justifying or legitimating role with respect to sociopolitical
institutions, procedures, and policies. Yet it is hardly controversial that, in various social-historical-cultural contexts, persons can reach all sorts of agreement: wise, prudent, just,
magnanimous, and kind agreements, as well as silly, unrealis-
tic, unjust, small-minded, and cruel ones. Furthermore, in some
contexts and with respect to some issues, it is virtually impossible to achieve unanimous agreement. With respect to such
cases, we typically want to make distinctions (which may themselves be controversial) about the comparative worthiness of the
reasons or causes for someone's withholding agreement. So it
is quite possible for actual sociopolitical consensus to develop
with respect to decisions that would not be morally supportable, according to the dictates of some theory (even some
liberal theory); and it is at least equally possible that actual
sociopolitical consensus would fail to develop with respect to
decisions that such a theory regards as desirable or obligatory.
In other words, the commitment of political liberalism to justi-

fying/legitimating a liberal set of principles, institutions, and attitudes typically turns out *not* to be a commitment to justifying/legitimating whatever citizens might actually agree to—even citizens in contemporary constitutional democracies. This would be to make liberal theory "political in the wrong way," to use Rawls's phrase.[15] Liberalism's task of justifying and legitimating, then, proves to be theory driven, at least to some degree. What gets legitimated by the theory in question seems to be only loosely and contingently related to actual sociopolitical consensus.

The appeal to theory suggests the other extreme (2), appeal to a particular religious, philosophical, or moral doctrine (i.e., Rawlsian comprehensive conception of the good). The problem with this alternative is political liberalism's commitment to the stance of neutrality. I have previously suggested that liberalism's historiographical conception of its own origins in sociopolitical compromise and consensus makes the idea of prescinding, in the public, political sphere, from what the parties to sociopolitical cooperations disagree about (e.g., comprehensive conceptions of the good) seem a quite rational and natural move. As I also stated, the stance of neutrality is suggested by the Rousseauian theoretical crystallization of concrete consensus in the idea of each identifying himself with all in making basic political decisions (determining *la volonté générale*). The Rousseauian identification of oneself with each is naturally interpreted as entailing the demand that each citizen, in participating in the political decision-making process, prescind from all that is peculiar to his situation—including religious, philosophical, or moral commitments that may fall into this category.

So, in order to justify, legitimate, and stabilize a certain set of liberal institutions—that is, to stop History—by the rules, indeed by liberalism's own rules, political liberalism needs some sort of 'neutral' mechanism, one that cannot be accused of appealing to religious, philosophical, or moral principles that are taken to be an expression of personal or partisan prepossession within the society in question. Yet, appeal to actual sociopolitical consensus does not seem to be a matter of stopping History at all, for sociopolitical consensus has a way of changing, both gradually and, on occasion, suddenly and dramatically. In fact, it is not clear that this latter empirical approach would leave much room for the construction of any political theory to which the terms "justifying," "legitimating," "stabilizing," "entrenching" could plausibly be applied. Perhaps the job of political philosophers and other theorists of the political could be supplanted by that of poll-takers, survey-researchers, and other data-driven social scientists!

Finding a *tertium quid* seems to be quite imperative for the political liberal. As I have indicated, some notion of practical rationality/reasonableness for the public or political sphere is the Great Hope. It would take a book of considerable length, learning, and subtlety to trace out in detail the history of the concept of practical rationality and the place of the liberal conception(s) of practical rationality, as applicable to the public, political sphere, within that history. Alasdair MacIntyre provides a succinct characterization of the traditional, preliberal idea of practical rationality and its connection with the human *telos*:

> Aquinas follows Aristotle in holding that the knowledge of our ultimate end, so far as it is within our rational powers to achieve, belongs to the theoretical rather than the practical activity of the intellect: "It must be said therefore that the practical intellect indeed has its *principium* [the translation of "*archē*"] in a universal consideration and in this respect is the same in subject as the theoretical intellect, but its consideration reaches its terminus in a particular thing which can be done" ([Aquinas], *Commentary on the Ethics*, VI, lect. 2). That is to say, we reason theoretically *to* and *about* that ultimate end which is the *archē* of practical enquiry and reasoning, but *from* that *archē* it is by practical reasoning that we are led to particular conclusions as to how to act.[16]

As we have seen, political liberalism is committed to severing the connection between practical rationality, at least as it is to be applied in the public, political sphere, and some determinate, thick conception of human beings' ultimate end or good. Thus, it would seem to require a more Kantian conception of practical rationality. However, simple universalizability, particularly empirical universalizability, does not seem to constitute a sufficient constraint on what is to count as an expression of practical rationality. In order to accomplish its mission of stopping History, justifying/legitimating a *particular* set of liberal principles, institutions, and practices (and, it is to be hoped, thus entrenching/stabilizing them), liberalism would seem to need a thicker, more substantive notion of practical rationality.

This situation issues in a sort of dilemma for political liberalism. A thin notion of practical rationality, such as one consisting in an empirical universalizability or *actual* consensus, is insufficient to allow political liberalism adequately to fulfill its justifying/legitimating (and entrenching/stabilizing) goal. But a thick notion that would be sufficient to accomplish such an end tends to compromise the stance of neutrality with respect to philosophical, religious, and moral diversity that political liberalism derives from its own historiography. In other words, the hope that practical rationality can ground a *tertium quid* between actual, piecemeal, and transitory compromises and modi vivendi, on the one hand, and appeal to some distinctive comprehensive conception of the good, on the other, turns out to be illusory. To illustrate this dilemma, I consider several attempts within contemporary political liberalism to make theoretical use of practical rationality and reasonableness.

The "ideal speech situation" or "ideally rational conversation" theory of Jürgen Habermas, Charles Larmore, et al., is one attempt to justify the stance of neutrality characteristic of political liberalism in terms of a notion of rationality. In the words of Larmore,

> The neutral justification of political neutrality is based upon what I believe is a universal norm of rational dialogue. When two people disagree about some specific point, but wish to continue talking about the more general problem they wish to solve, each should prescind from the beliefs that the other rejects, (1) in order to construct an argument on the basis of his other beliefs that will convince the other of the truth of the disputed belief, or (2) in order to shift to another aspect of the problem, where the possibilities of agreement seem greater. In the face of disagreement, those who wish to continue the conversation should retreat to *neutral ground*, with the hope of either resolving the dispute or of bypassing it.[17]

As Larmore recognizes, "it cannot be supposed that social life, and political activity in particular, is only conversation. *Die Weltgeschichte ist kein Weltseminar* [World history is not a world

discussion group]."[18] Yet the Rousseauian inference from the notion that political authority is equally vested in all citizens, viz., the idea that the moral legitimacy of at least basic political decisions rests in their ideal, rational justification to each citizen, can quite naturally manifest itself in such a conversational model of political legitimacy. As I remarked in the last chapter, this particular version of political liberalism seems to be more pragmatic (and, in a sense, populist) than some of its competitors. Larmore comments that

> political neutrality, as I have described it, is a relative matter. It does not require that the liberal state be neutral with respect to all conceptions of the good life, but only with respect to those actually disputed in the society. Where everyone agrees about some element of human flourishing, the liberal should have no reason to deny it a role in shaping political principles.[19]

Of course, such an abstract endorsement of an empirical solution to what can be taken as undisputed when we undertake our ideally rational political conversation does not explicitly address the issue of minority dissent: In a contemporary constitutional democracy of, say, a hundred million citizens, does one holdout (or several hundred, or several thousand, or a hundred thousand) vitiate the consensus? Nonetheless, this particular variety of political liberalism would seem to remain more firmly attached, at least in principle, than several competing varieties to the historical roots of liberalism in *actual* compromise and consensus.

The idea of a retreat to neutral ground may initially seem, when considered from a sufficiently abstract and schematic perspective, to be an obviously rational and reasonable move when political decisions are being made in contexts of pluralism of the sort assumed by contemporary political liberalism. But further consideration of the dynamics of political decision making, even as idealized by such a conversational model, tends to undermine this initial impression. If it were assumed that retreat to neutral ground by the parties to such a political conversation amounted to retreat to some set of logically powerful first principles or *axioms*, from which more particular sociopolitical consequences could be deduced as consequences, the picture would be a compelling one indeed. For, then, construction of cogent deductive arguments from such shared premises that could resolve disputed issues would, in principle, be a straightforward matter. However, it is clear that the sort of practical rationality applicable to resolving sociopolitical issues typically is not of this axiomatic-deductive sort—as was recognized by even those pre-liberal thinkers (such as Aristotle and Aquinas) who tended to regard practical reasoning as closely analogous to theoretical reasoning.

Even if it were assumed that the neutral ground that is staked out by prescinding from controversial or disputed beliefs is constituted by some very general moral and sociopolitical principles, it is not clear that much would follow from those principles—particularly cogent arguments "that will convince the other[s] of the truth of the disputed belief[s]" to be resolved in order to obtain a politically useful consensus. Actual contingent political compromise and consensus is usually something of a grab bag: It typically consists of provisional and limited agreements about different sorts of sociopolitical matters at different levels of generality and importance. In fact, common sense suggests that agreement might often be most easily obtained about relatively peripheral matters that do not directly impinge on issues of deep principle. Where, in a constitutional democracy such as the United States, there seems to be a fair degree of consensus on fundamental principles, those principles often turn out to be platitudes ("equal opportunity is important," "we must retain religious freedom," "due process is a central desideratum in police and judicial procedures"). Depending on what larger conceptual framework or comprehensive conception of the good they are fitted into, such principles are platitudes in the sense that they are susceptible to such different interpretations with such radically different consequences that the pragmatic sociopolitical import of agreement on them often amounts to very little. I would assume that most of those citizens belonging to the 'Religious Right' (to use the name adopted by the American media) and liberal Protestants, traditional Catholics, libertarians, and secular liberals all are willing (perhaps for very different reasons) to give assent to the First-Amendment provision that "Congress shall make no law respecting an establishment of religion, or prohibiting the free exercise thereof." But it is surely the case that recent skirmishes in America's culture wars indicate that agreement on this principle has minimal import with respect to the issue of the proper place of religion in public life.

It is also not always the case that retreat to common conceptual ground constitutes the adoption of a neutral stance with respect to competing positions. Imagine someone trying to arbitrate the logical dispute between mathematical intuitionists and classical, nonintuitionists by suggesting that they retreat to the common logical ground on which they can agree. Although mathematicians are perhaps not well known for their practical acumen, few nonintuitionists are going to be particularly grateful for this assistance: Because the logic accepted by intuitionists is a proper part of that accepted by classical nonintuitionists, this move essentially resolves the dispute in favor of the former. Really important and at issue in the dispute is what the parties do not have in common; and the fact they are willing to agree to some logical principles does not provide the materials for resolving their differences. Similarly, the retreat to common ground typically favors those who are committed to less rather than to more in a political dispute. The political functions that contemporary libertarians take to be legitimate typically are also taken to be legitimate by most varieties of nonlibertarian. Retreat to common ground here is really retreat to libertarian ground, and such a move would seem to advance the political debate between libertarians and their opponents very little.

In sum, I submit that the ideally rational conversation model does not really accomplish much in terms of grounding any liberal political theory. Of course, commonsensical considerations suggest that political action in a constitutional democracy is most feasible and perhaps most likely to be successful where fairly wide support for it can be mustered. But such areas of agreement typically will be piecemeal and theoretically unsystematic in the absence of any unifying *Weltanschauung* (comprehensive conception of the world). I suspect that a deeper, more principled or theoretical accord is often achieved, in those circumstances where it is achieved, not by retreat to supposedly neutral ground but by different comprehensive conceptions and different sets of basic principles all jostling against one another. Moving from disagreement to agreement at the deeper, more principled or theoretical level—where it does occur—is more often a matter of paradigm-shift or alteration of *Gestalt*.

So the "reasoning together" typical in the moral and sociopolitical sphere, from Isaias to LBJ and beyond, is either this sort of conceptual encounter or a matter of purely pragmatic, piecemeal agreements where we can find them, and on whatever basis that we can effect them, when doing so seems useful.

In his *Political Liberalism*, Rawls distinguishes practical rationality and reasonableness. The former concept is an epistemological one pertaining to finding appropriate means to further given ends: it pertains to the "powers of judgment and deliberation in seeking ends and interests peculiarly [belonging to a single, unified agent]."[20] But it also pertains to the ability of agents to "balance final ends by their significance for their plan of life as a whole, and by how well these ends cohere with and complement one another" (51). Reasonableness, on the other hand, proves to be an essentially moral rather than epistemological notion for Rawls, and is not reducible to rationality. It is, in its "first aspect," the "form of moral sensibility that underlies the desire to engage in fair [i.e., based on egalitarian symmetry assumptions] cooperation as such, and to do so on terms that others as equals might reasonably be expected to endorse (51). A "second basic aspect" of the concept of reasonableness defined by Rawls is the "willingness to recognize the burdens of judgment and to accept their consequences for the use of public reason in directing the legitimate exercise of political power in a constitutional regime" (54). Recall that, for Rawls, the "burdens of judgment" are those theoretical and practical epistemological considerations that make it difficult (or impossible) for citizens in a contemporary constitutional democracy to come to agreement concerning a comprehensive conception of the good.

Much liberal theory is built into Rawls's notion of reasonableness. The first aspect of reasonableness, the "desire to engage in fair cooperation *as such*, and to do so on terms that others as equals might reasonably be expected to endorse [emphasis added]," really lies at the heart of the abstract liberal, Rousseauian conception of distributive justice that we have previously considered. The Rousseauian idea of distributive justice is that, because each citizen shares equally in the authority of sociopolitical organization, each should be equally able to endorse any legitimate activity of the state—from his impersonal and public perspective as a *citoyen*. The willingness

always to cooperate on egalitarian terms as such, i.e., indepen-
dently of the particularities of one's own interests, goals, or
conception of the good, perhaps makes some sense (as "reasonable") within this very abstract, theoretical context. The virtue
depicted is perhaps best represented as fair-spiritedness
proper to games or sport—the virtue behind sportsmanlike conduct. Free and equal players, or potential players, will play to
win—to advance their or their team's ends and interests. But
all players should be prepared to accept a set of rules and abide
by them, irrespective of the particular advantage or disadvantage of doing so and, indeed, irrespective of what game/sport
is to be played or what the point of the game is. The rules of
the game should be mutually justifiable to all the (potential)
players, of course; if this is not so, if there is not agreement
about the rules, there is not a single game being played but, at
best, a number of simultaneous games.

What Rawls, in effect, does is to transfer this notion of fair
play to political society's players, or their suitably idealized and
veiled representatives, and thus make it foundational to his
notion of distributive justice (as fairness). The idea of privileging cooperation, above other ends that might be furthered
within the political sphere, in terms of mutually justifiable rules
or principles is thus central to Rawls's notion of reasonableness. Surely Rawls is correct in thinking that common
agreement on the basis of cooperation is a social virtue. And
a modicum of such agreement with respect to *procedural*
issues is probably necessary to get much of anything done. But
Rawls's notions of reasonableness and of public reason clearly
goes beyond the procedural: They require an agreement to cooperate on a basis that clearly differentiates the "right from the
"good" and that eschews any public appeal to one's conception of the good, of what is of fundamental worth with respect
to human existence, at least with respect to "constitutional essentials or basic questions of justice" (62). However, in actual
sociopolitical intercourse, it seems reasonable to suppose that
other ends to be achieved by sociopolitical action (e.g., certain
constituents of one's comprehensive conception of the good)
sometimes trump the end of engaging only in some idealized
form of mutually justifiable cooperation *per se*—i.e., at any
price, relative to one's comprehensive conception. To consider
an alternative picture (to which I shall return in chapter 4),

perhaps political life in a contemporary constitutional democracy should be viewed simply as an empirical concurrence of a number of different "games," with rather different *substantive* ends and rules, but with limited agreement about certain procedural matters pertaining to how one uses the playing field.

It is not obvious how detailed and determinate the consequences of the second aspect of the Rawlsian conception of reasonableness are. At a general level, when this aspect of reasonableness is incorporated into Rawls's notion of public reason (which should govern the deportment of citizens in the public, political arena), the result is a moral requirement of citizens to prescind from their particular comprehensive conceptions of the good when acting the rôle of *citoyen*, at least when "constitutional essentials and basic questions of justice" are at issue. This requirement nicely accords with the Rousseauian application of the principle of distributive justice: The equal sharing of all citizens in political authority dictates that any fundamental political decision be ideally justified/justifiable in terms of the interchangeable *amour de soi-même* of the citizens, so that each can rationally equate herself or himself with any arbitrary citizen in voting. However, it is far from clear that such a liberal conception of reasonableness has exclusive claim to the term.

As I suggested in chapter 2, the proof of the pudding lies in just what is included in the notion *amour de soi-même*—just what, with respect to the interest of citizens, is to be equally respected, protected, and furthered in the political sphere. This question is more-or-less extensionally equivalent to the question of just what Rawls believes to be the sociopolitical consequences of the application of rationality and reasonableness in the form of his public reason. Here the dilemma to which I referred some pages ago reemerges. If too much content is built into the notion of public reason, so that it will have some rather determinate consequences with respect to actual political issues, the pretense of the neutrality of the application of public reason becomes quite difficult to sustain.

Public reason, like any other kind of reason, must have some first principles, either explicitly stated or tacitly presupposed. And, as with other forms of reason, in order to get more consequences out, one must put more assumptions or first principles in. These will look very much like just those philosophical,

moral, and religious assumptions that are constitutive of a comprehensive conception of the good. According to the typical
assumption made by theorists of political liberalism (such as
Rawls) concerning the ineliminable pluralism of contemporary
constitutional democracies, such assumptions will be controversial. Yet, if one attempts to make the notion of public reason
as thin and neutral as possible, it is not clear that one can
derive from it anything close to the full panoply of liberal principles, institutions, and attitudes with which liberal theorists
generally wish to stop History—i.e., to justify/legitimate theoretically (and, it is to be hoped, to stabilize/entrench). That
is, it seems quite difficult to construct a substantive liberal political theory that is not partisan. A more-or-less neutral theory
will typically be too thin to serve the purposes of a liberal
justifying/legitimating theory. This dilemma is manifest is some
recent commentary on the Rawlsian notions of rationality/
reasonableness and of their instantiation in public reason.

  Gary Leedes maintains that Rawls's constraints of public
reason, as enshrined in what Leedes calls the "LPC" (the "liberal political conception"), do not at all promote the stance of
neutrality with respect to the influence of religion in the public sphere:

> Rawls treats religious speech as an aggressive and divisive mode
> of communication that must be confined to the private sphere. This
> kind of discriminatory treatment is unlikely to end the culture wars
> between many Americans and their adversaries including Chris-
> tian fundamentalists, conservative Catholics, and Orthodox Jews.
> Rawls is in cloud-cuckoo land if he thinks that religious disagree-
> ments will be reduced in number by a political theory that stig-
> matizes devout persons whose political opinions are consistently
> aligned with their religious orientation.[21]

To put Leedes's point in somewhat different terms, it seems
clear that Rawls's notion of public reason is not neutral (at least
not neutral "in effect"[22]) among various religious traditions that
enjoy some degree of popular support—even if we limit ourselves to consideration of Western constitutional democracies.
Rawls's LPC and the conception of public reason that under-
girds it favor those liberal, quasi-modernist, and partially secularized Protestant, Catholic, Jewish, and Islamic traditions that
can manage to accommodate to their world view, as a semi-

independent module, the sort of generic theoretical liberalism that is the LPC. This result is not surprising because more traditional religious orientations tend, at some juncture, to come into conflict with liberal principles. But this fact is nonetheless disturbing to some liberal theorists because it makes it so clear that political liberalism (e.g., as instantiated in the Rawlsian notions of rationality and reasonableness and public reason) really constitutes a philosophical or moral theory that is "on all fours" with other *Weltanschauungen* or comprehensive conceptions of the good—and thus does *not* constitute some neutral theoretical device of arbitration among such conceptions.

In response to Leedes, Lawrence Solum maintains that Rawls really is (or, at least, should be) committed to an "inclusive ideal of public reason" rather than an "exclusive" one.[23] Solum dismisses what he terms a laissez-faire conception of public reason (which "interprets the idea of public reason as reason that is free of constraint") as a "live option for our political culture" because such a conception would violate what I have been referring to as the Rousseauian principle and what Solum refers to as the "liberal principle" of legitimacy.[24] Basic political decisions should ideally be capable of being endorsed by all citizens "in light of principles and ideals acceptable to them as reasonable and rational."[25] It is clear that, in the view of Solum (and most political liberals), this principle requires a restriction on the content of public reason, i.e., a restriction on what sorts of premise and what kinds of argument can legitimately (morally) be invoked in the public sphere when political decisions are being made. (I assume that even a laissez-faire conception would permit constraints on the form—e.g., time, place, manner—of expression of at least some kinds of public, political discourse.)

An exclusive ideal of public reason would morally deny citizens a right to appeal to premises or kinds of argument—ones, for example, drawn from their particular world-views or conceptions of the good—that all other citizens (idealized as rational and reasonable, in the Rawlsian sense) could not be expected to share. An inclusive ideal of public reason favored by Solum would (morally) permit citizens to appeal to "nonpublic reasons"; "[b]ut nonpublic reasons would only be allowed if sufficient public reasons were also given." This doctrine is interpreted by Solum as implying "that nonpublic reasons could only be given in two circumstances: (1) if the nonpublic reasons were the foundation for a public reason, and (2) if the nonpublic reason were an additional sufficient reason for a policy that would be given an independent and sufficient justification by a public reason."[26]

Although Solum seems to regard his endorsement of this inclusive ideal of public reason a sort of concession to those whose political views, to paraphrase Leedes, are "consistently aligned with their moral, philosophical, or religious orientation," it obviously is not much of a concession. Such a notion of public reason remains an attempt to limit morally the political playing field not just procedurally (with respect to legislative and judicial practices and institutions associated with liberal constitutional democracies) but substantively. In particular, at the center of any plausible variant of Rawls's concept of public reason will be a distinctive moral and philosophical doctrine of political liberalism—a doctrine that is controversial even in contemporary Western constitutional democracies: the right is to be distinguished from the good and the influence of the latter, insofar as possible, is to be excluded from the public, political sphere.

Rawls's conception of public reason is supposed to capture the Rousseauian notion of political legitimacy—a notion of universal, rational and reasonable endorsement of or consent to at least important and basic political decisions. The invocation of rationality and reasonableness here means that this is not a purely empirical notion of consent or endorsement, because actual endorsement/consent, or the withholding of it, will often involve the sort of particularity that liberalism, or at least political liberalism, wishes to eliminate from public, political life. But the abstract, Rousseauian conception of legitimacy, although it represents a distinctively liberal philosophical stance about the relation between sociopolitical institutions and the conception of the human good, typically does not issue in determinate recommendations with respect to more-or-less concrete sociopolitical issues. As I have previously suggested, to justify/legitimate a determinate liberal sociopolitical program an account is needed of what aspects of human life and what sorts of behavior merit equal respect, protection, and promotion in the form of freedoms, rights, and other forms of institutionalized political action. All of this may be built into a thick, content-driven conception of public reason. But, then, it will be all the more obvious that the notion of public reason is not really the neutral conceptual device that it was supposed to be and that its application really involves privileging a more-or-less comprehensive conception of the good, or related group of such conceptions. Yet, the attempt to keep the notion of public reason as procedural and neutral as possible—although this attempt still yields a distinctively liberal conceptual framework with respect to the relationship between person as *citoyen* and as *bourgeois*—has the effect of diminishing the usefulness of the concept in terms of the goal of stopping History by the justification/legitimation (and stabilization/entrenchment) of a *determinate* set of liberal institutions, principles, and attitudes.

A good example of this tension arises with respect to a much discussed footnote in Rawls's *Political Liberalism*. While he typically presents his conceptions of rationality and reasonableness and of public reason as neutral, consensus-forming conceptual tools, he maintains in the note in question that "any comprehensive doctrine that leads to a balance of political values excluding that duly qualified right [to procure an abortion] in the first trimester is to that extent unreasonable."[27] Although this conclusion is (after a fashion) supported by some claims (e.g., "at this early stage of pregnancy the political value of the equality of women is overriding" [the two 'competing' political values of "due respect for human life" and the "ordered reproduction of political society over time"]), Rawls provides no argument that I can discern that this particular interpretation of the correct balance of political values follows from his conceptions of reasonableness or of public reason. It is certainly true, however, that some sort of right to abort has become a part of most political programs that are termed "liberal" in the United States and other contemporary constitutional democracies.

This tension with respect to the Rawlsian notions of reasonableness and public reason has been discussed in rather more general terms by Peter de Marneffe. He points out that Rawls's notion of public reason really contains two constituent ideas: with respect to the exercise of political power (at least with respect to What Is Really Important), (1) citizens should take only those positions "that are supported by *values that every reasonable citizen could endorse*," and (2) "citizens should take only those positions that are supported by *liberal political values*."[28] As de Marneffe points out, (1) and (2) are equivalent if every reasonable citizen could be expected to support all and only liberal political values. Reasonably enough, de Marneffe is concerned whether this assumption is true. One tactic for achieving equivalence would be to weaken the notion of a particular set of values supporting a particular political position, and de Marneffe tries this. According to a conception of "adequately defended" introduced by him, it would follow that a political "position is adequately defended *in terms of liberal political values*, then, if it is able to answer all the relevant questions [such a position] raises solely in terms of liberal political values at least as well as the contrary position is able to answer all the relevant questions it raises solely in terms of liberal political values" (240).

This sense of adequately defended is, I believe, so weak as to be Pickwickian. It follows from this conception that although some of what are thought to be distinctively liberal positions on political issues (prescription of some form of abortion on demand) are adequately defended solely by liberal values, it may well happen that the contrary position on the same issue (e.g., the proscription of abortion on demand) is also adequately defended by exclusive appeal to the same values. It would seem more consonant with our ordinary notion of what it means for a position to be rationally supported or adequately defended by some theory or set of values to say that, for such an issue, liberal values are in themselves silent: They fail either to support or to oppose either of the contrary positions on such a political issue. It would thus transpire that the answer is negative to de Marneffe's question "whether every position on the scope of basic liberty that is central to contemporary liberalism can be defended" "by appeal to liberal political values alone" (239).

De Marneffe himself comes to a very similar conclusion by introducing a stronger notion, that of a position on a political issue being "adequately supported by liberal political values on a *fully reasonable interpretation* of these values." He suggests that perhaps Rawlsian public reason only sets bounds for positions on political issues such that a position falls within those bounds if there is some defensible interpretation of liberal values that really supports it, outside if there is no such interpretation. However, it would then be the case that public reason "cannot show us that the only reasonable positions are those that are fully reasonable from the liberal point of view" (246–47). Consequently, de Marneffe concludes that

> Rawls has not yet specified the content of public reason in such a way that it clearly supports all and only those positions on the scope of basic liberty that are fully reasonable from the liberal point of view. This is because he has not yet identified a method of interpreting liberal political values that yields only interpretations that support these liberal positions (248).

It might initially seem that the problem that engages de Marneffe results merely from a conflation of two senses of liberalism: (1) a popular, media sense of the term connoting a particular party orientation in American and European politics that is opposed to conservatism and (2) a more abstract, theoretical position represented both by the political theory of classical liberal thinkers (e.g., Locke and John Stuart Mill and, perhaps, Rousseau and Kant) and by that of contemporary political liberals (e.g., Rawls, Dworkin, Habermas). It is perhaps not surprising that not all the items on the agenda of liberalism in sense (1) should be entailed or be otherwise straightforwardly supported by a political theory that is liberal in sense (2). However, as I have previously suggested, a theory of political liberalism that is Rousseauian in the sense of deriving political legitimacy from some form of idealized universal consent will be sufficiently abstract as to not address many political issues the resolutions of which depend upon judgments concerning the aspects of human life that merit equal political respect, protection, and promotion and those concerning the appropriate balance of competing claims based on these values. Some filling in must be done in order to derive anything approaching a determinate political program. And the two obvious sources are (1) moral, philosophical, or religious assumptions (i.e., constituents of comprehensive conceptions of the good) of a theoretical, perfectionist character and (2) the outcome(s) of actual, contingent sociopolitical consensus. Because political liberalism—and, in general, liberalism founded on the Rousseauian conception of political legitimacy—has good theoretical reason for eschewing support from source (1), source (2) remains.

As we have seen, source (2)—appeal to actual public consensus—accords well with liberalism's own favored historiography. A good case can be made that many items of the agenda of liberalism referred to by de Marneffe as "controversial liberal positions" are the result of liberalism's assimilating a variety of social movements that managed to gain substantial popular support—e.g., the antislavery movement, religious indifferentism, economic egalitarianism (although that desideratum originated not so much with liberalism but with more radical socialist and Marxist political thought), the sexual revolution, the civil rights movement, and feminism. Perhaps the historiographical picture of the roots of liberalism in compromise, consensus, and modi vivendi gives the liberal tradition its often rather Whiggish character: It is common for liberal theorists to assume that, by and large, such popular movements are on the right moral and sociopolitical track. Yet, with the exception of the antislavery movement, these particular popular movements have not yet achieved anything close to complete consensus—otherwise, the liberal positions issuing from them would not be controversial. And the liberal tradition has generally wanted to appropriate only those movements that it regards as progressive. For example, the political renascence of what the American media have termed the Religious Right is certainly a popular movement that most political liberals have regarded as something of a Bogeyperson.

In fact, the dynamic that obtains between liberal theory (more specifically, that which is politically mandated by liberalism) and the content of various popular, or quasi-popular, social movements is complex. This dynamic represents one aspect of the relationship between liberalism and democracy, a relationship that has long been recognized as containing its own tensions. An interesting case of the interaction between quasi-popular, progressive movements and liberal theory arises in connection with Ronald Dworkin's advocacy of "liberalism based on equality," which "takes as fundamental that government treat its citizens as equals, and insists on moral neutrality only to the degree that equality requires it."[29] This

egalitarian basis of liberalism is, Dworkin argues, to be preferred to "liberalism based on neutrality," which "takes as fundamental the idea that the government must not take sides on
moral issues, and . . . supports only such egalitarian measures
as can be shown to be the result of that principle."[30] At least
part of the reason for Dworkin's preference of liberalism based
on equality to liberalism based on neutrality is his conviction
that the former can more easily justify various of the more in-
terventionist items on many contemporary liberal political agen-
das: e.g., some forms of economic redistribution and affirmative
action programs. What is unclear is whether his choice of theoretical basis should be viewed (1) as a deeper and more per-
spicuous theoretical working out of a liberal *Weltanschauung*
present from the beginning of the tradition, so to speak, or
(2) as an alteration in the substantive theoretical core of liberalism in response to pressure from progressive movements that are deemed, for whatever reasons, deserving of
political support.

Among theorists of political liberalism, Rawls has perhaps
been most creative in attempting to construct a *tertium quid* to
serve as the theoretical political justification/legitimation of
institutions, principles, and attitudes judged worthy of liberal
support. He has attempted to avoid the "absolutist" foundation of liberalism in a philosophical, moral, or religious *Weltanschauung* because of his conviction that doing so would vitiate
the public justification/legitimation associated with the Rousseauian conception of political legitimacy in idealized universal endorsement or consent. But, he has attempted to avoid the
other "extreme" of turning the liberal notion of justification/
legitimation into whatever is yielded by the democratic process of actual formation of compromise and modi vivendi. Such
concrete political agreement cannot be trusted always to issue
in results in conformity with the general tenor of liberal political thought. Moreover, it seems unlikely that such concrete
political compromise and agreement could really yield the
sort of justification/legitimation (let alone stabilization/
entrenchment) to which theorists of political liberalism have
generally aspired. The sought-for *tertium quid* or *via media* (middle path) is to be delimited by such notions as "shared
political culture of a democratic society," "rationality/reason-
ableness," and "public reason."

A conception of reasonableness that, in effect, embodies the Rousseauian, liberal ideal of political legitimacy—although itself representing a nonneutral moral/philosophical assumption—goes some distance toward the goal of stopping History at a liberal juncture by means of theory. But the present discussion suggests that it does not go very far. Sweet reasonableness, whether that of Isaias, LBJ, or Rawls, seems unsuited to the task of justifying/legitimating, in the public way desired by theorists of political liberalism, a full liberal agenda.

In political practice, and even at a fairly rarefied and theoretical level of the consideration of political practice, the liberal tradition probably represents a dynamic balance of the claims of developing popular movements and consensuses and those of some more general view of man, society, and political organization that developed, with variations, in the post-Reformation, Enlightenment milieu of western Europe. The dilemma of contemporary political liberalism, however, with its requirement of a public justifying/legitimating theory, is that a general liberal view of man, society, and political organization is not thick enough to support such an enterprise of justification. At the same time, a forthright Whiggish appeal to the development of a lineage of progressive popular movements, which it is hoped will eventually emulate the antislavery movement—although without a bloody civil war—and lead to consensus, may seem to amount to a renunciation of the justificatory enterprise altogether.

One option is for the liberal tradition to retain its goal of justifying/legitimating but give up the notion that such an enterprise should be distinctively public or political, i.e., appeal to premises and modes of reasoning that should, in principle, be acceptable to all rational and reasonable citizens. This would amount to at least an implicit admission that the justifying/legitimating enterprise is perfectionist and, in that sense, "partisan"—that, in the words of Margaret Moore quoted at the end of chapter 1, "[l]iberalism is a conception of the good, on all fours with other conceptions of the good, and deeply antithetical to many moral and religious conceptions."[31] Here I would reiterate: The fact that many forms of liberalism advocate, as a political value, principles and institutions that leave a good deal of room for individual choice and development regarding select forms of behavior does not mean that liberalism does not rely upon a conception of the human good or of what is worthwhile about human existence. In making some kinds of autonomy or freedom an important part of what is worthwhile in human life—and a value to be guaranteed by sociopolitical organization—liberalism simply comes to embrace a conception of the good that is not, in all respects, as determinate or comprehensive as certain competing conceptions.

In effect—whether or not in intention—the appeal to such notions as public reason, rationality, and reasonableness by theorists of political liberalism may sometimes be a quite partisan rhetorical ploy. These notions are to be interpreted by socioeconomic and cultural elites (in the media, government, the judiciary, and academia) in such a way as to screen out certain kinds of argument and to dismiss some potential players as not having the proper moral, intellectual, or social credentials for participating in public, democratic "conversation." So from *this* perspective—as a partisan rhetorical strategy—the invocation of some conception of public rationality as a sociopolitical ideal certainly might not be futile. But, of course, this is not the way in which such an ideal is officially conceptualized in liberal theory.[32]

Another possibility, perhaps, is for liberalism to give up the strategy of attempting to legitimize and stabilize (in terms of a comprehensive public theory and public virtues, which are supposed to be accorded moral pride of place in the public life of society) and to return to its historical roots in concrete sociopolitical compromise, modi vivendi, and consensus wherever it can be found. This "return to democratic roots" would not pay particular regard to a theory of justification/legitimation (or of stabilization/entrenchment) that is public or political in the sense attached to these terms by such theorists of political liberalism as Rawls. Citizens might or might not develop their own more-or-less elaborated political theories fitting with their particular *Weltanschauungen* or more-or-less comprehensive conceptions of the good in a variety of ways. In some cases, making items of principle or theory part of the subject-matter of political debate, compromise, and search for modus vivendi might prove to be necessary or useful. But there would be no expectation that such a process would issue in an overarching liberal political theory that all rational and reasonable citizens could be expected to endorse. And there certainly would be no assumption that achieving such theoretical concord is an overriding moral imperative in the political sphere. I return to this suggestion in the next and final chapter. However, I shall now have something to say about several civic virtues of central importance to the liberal political tradition.

Liberal versus Non-Liberal Niceness: Tolerance and Civility

We are all familiar with those traits of character and modes of behavior that lubricate the machinery of social interaction: a degree of agreeableness and affability, politeness, reticence in asserting one's own claims or attempting to have one's own way in nonessential matters, a readiness to show respect toward others, a sensitivity toward their feelings, and the ability to consider issues from their point of view. Most persons would agree that the proper development and exercise of these character traits is to some degree difficult and involves a nicety of judgment that results from a complex combination of disposition, socialization, and effort that is not simply a matter of the acceptance of some general principles or rules and the straightforward application of them (or of their deductive consequences) in particular circumstances. Further, most of us do not always live up to the standards that we accept with respect to the exercise of these particular social virtues. The most common failures here are ones of deficiency. But failures of excess are certainly possible. These are discussed by Plutarch under the term "compliancy" (*dysōpia*), which, he says, "turns aside from justice those rendering verdicts, silences those involved in deliberations, and makes persons say and do many things unwillingly."[33] A noteworthy literary example of *dysōpia* is the character Mrs. Dempster in Robertson Davies's novel *Fifth Business*; she is missing and then is discovered by her parson husband (and accompanying search party) with a tramp in the midst of the act of adultery, whereupon she responds to her husband's inquiry concerning her motivation with the explanation, "He was very civil, 'Masa. And he wanted it so badly."[34] Of course, how one regards such social virtues as civility and tolerance in application (and what one takes to be excess and defect with respect to their practice) will likely depend on the larger view of human life in which they are embedded. For the orthodox Christian, these issues are inseparable from considerations involving the virtues of humility and self-abnegation and the cardinal theological virtue of *caritas* (unsatisfactorily translated as either "charity" or "love"), as well as the virtue of justice. Not surprisingly, the same is not true for Plutarch.

When we move from the personal and associational to the public and political sphere, such social virtues still have their place. The question is just what that place is. The liberal political tradition has developed a very particular, characteristic answer to this question, one that is fundamentally at odds with a more traditional viewpoint, which I shall, in due course, recommend. Within the liberal tradition, the practice of such social virtues as toleration and civility becomes a mandate of distributive justice. The liberal may adhere to the doctrine of political liberalism that interprets distributive justice as enjoining a public and political stance of neutrality regarding conceptions of the good, or he or she may adhere to the perfectionist conception of distributive justice as enjoining the equal guarantee to citizens of autonomy in general or the equal guarantee of some select set of liberties as the requisite means for fleshing in and living out their own individual conceptions of what is worthwhile in life. In either case, liberal distributive justice mandates public and political 'toleration' for conceptions of the good, attitudes, and types of speech and behavior within publicly prescribed limits that may be reprobated 'privately' (i.e., when we are wearing our *bourgeois* or *homme* hat, as opposed to our *citoyen* one). And, at least for Rawls, the social virtue of civility is co-opted by his interpretation of the requirement of distributive justice that we seek to eliminate from the public and political realm those aspects of comprehensive conceptions of the good that do not support liberal political values. There is, he says, "a moral, not a legal, duty—the duty of civility—to be able to explain to one another on those fundamental questions how the principles and policies they advocate and vote for can be supported by the [liberal] political values of public reason."[35]

In effect, the subsumption of toleration, civility, and related civil virtues of restraint under a liberal conception of distribu-

tive justice mandates a moral responsibility, as a matter of justice, to 'tolerate' what one holds to be fundamentally wrong
moral, philosophical, and religious principles. In contrast,
Joseph Raz comes closer to the traditional view in suggesting
that "[t]oleration is a distinctive moral virtue only if it curbs
desires, inclinations and convictions which are thought by the
tolerant person to be in themselves desirable."[36] A common
mistake, says Raz, is that "[p]eople who come to realize that
their intolerant tendencies have to be curbed may conclude that
they are bad in themselves, rather than merely in their expression."[37] A recent writer on the issue of religious liberty,
Michael Davies, succinctly summarizes an essential feature of
what I have termed the "traditional view" of tolerance: "The
state is bound in justice to accord a citizen what he possesses
as a right. It is only what cannot be demanded as a right that
can be conceded as an act of toleration."[38] Toleration, then, is
essentially a matter of prudence—a strongly context-dependent,
and not necessarily algorithmic, decision not to oppose or re-
monstrate against what intrinsically merits opposition or remon-
stration. What is sometimes termed "dogmatic intolerance" is
a virtue. In the words of Bernard Häring,

> *First Principle:* No one may tolerate error in principle.
> This form of tolerance, which we call dogmatic tolerance, is
> evil. We must defend dogmatic intolerance, the intolerance direct-
> ed to error as such and in principle. 'Total hostility to error' (*Er-
> rores interficite*) . . .
>   But every genuine and sincere conviction creates an impa-
> tience with error, is intolerant of error as such. Theoretic or dog-
> matic tolerance implies as much as indifference, scepticism, total
> absence of conviction, denial of the faith. But authentic intoler-
> ance demands a humble and honest investigation of one's own
> cherished convictions. Are they truly matters of faith, and do we
> formulate them with due prudence and circumspection?[39]

However, there may be very good prudential reason to accord personal or civic toleration to the erring. Refraining from
judgments about the sincerity and ultimate moral state of others is perhaps more a matter of justice than toleration, in the
strict sense I have just distinguished. Häring is but reiterating
traditional Catholic teaching when he states that the "domain
of subjective convictions is entirely beyond our power to judge.

Here we should follow the directive of our Lord: 'Do not judge, that you may not be judged!' (Mt 7:1)."[40]

But toleration of various sorts of behavior may also be desirable or even morally mandatory—even though that behavior is intrinsically erroneous, vicious, or evil—in order to secure a greater good or deter a worse evil. As St. Thomas Aquinas puts it,

> [H]uman government is derived from the divine government and ought to emulate it. God, although He is omnipotent and entirely good, nonetheless permits certain evils which he could prevent to come to be in the universe lest, if they were eliminated, greater goods would be eliminated or even worse evils would ensue. Thus, therefore, in human government those who are in charge rightly tolerate certain evils lest certain goods be impeded or worse evils be incurred: thus Augustine says in the second book of his *de Ordine*, "take away prostitutes from the human order and you will throw everything into disorder with lust." Consequently, although unbelievers sin in their rites, they may be tolerated either on account of some good that comes to be from them or on account of some evil that is avoided.[41]

In the late nineteenth century Pope Leo XIII developed guidelines for limited Catholic accommodation with and participation in liberal constitutional democracies:

> Yet, with the discernment of a true mother, the Church weighs the great burden of human weakness, and well knows the course down which the minds and actions of men are in this our age being borne. For this reason, while not conceding any right to anything save what is true and honest, she does not forbid public authority to tolerate what is at variance with truth and justice, for the sake of avoiding some greater evil or of obtaining or preserving some greater good. God Himself, in His providence though infinitely good and powerful permits evil to exist in the world, partly that greater good may not be impeded, and partly that greater evil may not ensue. In the government of States, it is not forbidden to imitate the Ruler of the world; and, as the authority of man is powerless to prevent every evil, it has (as St. Augustine says) *to overlook and leave unpunished many things which are punished, and rightly, by divine Providence.* But if, in such circumstances, for the sake of the common good (and this is the only legitimate reason), human law may or even should tolerate evil, it may not and should not approve or desire evil for its own sake . . .

But, to judge aright, we must acknowledge that the more a State is driven to tolerate evil the further is it from perfection; and that tolerance of evil which is dictated by political prudence should be strictly confined to the limits which its justifying cause, the public welfare, requires. Wherefore, if such tolerance would be injurious to the public welfare, and entail greater evils on the State, it would not be lawful; for in such case the motive of good is wanting. And although in the extraordinary condition of these times the Church usually acquiesces in certain modern liberties, not because she prefers them in themselves, but because she judges it expedient to permit them, she would in happier times exercise her own liberty; and by persuasion, exhortation, and entreaty, would endeavor, as she is bound, to fulfill the duty assigned to her by God of providing for the eternal salvation of mankind. One thing, however, remains always true—that liberty which is claimed for all to do all things is not, as We have often said, of itself desirable, inasmuch as it is contrary to reason that error and truth should have equal rights.[42]

Let us briefly consider two rather different instances of toleration. Following received doctrine, Leo XIII teaches in this same encyclical that "civil society must acknowledge God as its Founder and Parent, and must obey and reverence His power and authority. Justice therefore forbids, and reason itself forbids, the State to be godless."[43] It follows, therefore, that a form of polity that does not support authentic Christian *cultus* is deficient in the distinctly political virtue of justice—in this case, justice toward God. However, in a situation of religious pluralism, there may be sufficient reason to permit or even require some policy of religious neutrality or indifferentism. The "sufficient reason" will appeal to greater goods to be achieved (e.g., amity requisite for the effective pursuit of other aspects of the common good) or worse evils to be avoided (civil disturbance, avoidance of occasions of cruelty that a climate of civil repression might provide, disinclination to provide martyrs in witness to moral or religious error). In, say, the contemporary United States, such prudential, consequentialist considerations seem to be overwhelming. I know of no American Catholic, no matter how traditional or conservative, who supports the repeal of the First Amendment to the Constitution. But it is natural and reasonable that, from this Catholic perspective, the American tradition of separation of Church and State will be regarded as open to interpretation and modification—as indeed the establishment clause in fact has been interpreted and redefined. The proponent of the view I have been discussing will naturally want to use social and political means to bring this liberal tradition into as close harmony with the demands of justice and the claims of the truth as prudential considerations permit. But the justice that is relevant here is not the liberal notion of political justice that mandates a principled toleration, grounded in rights, of some range of expression (or nonexpression) of religiosity.

According to the traditional understanding of toleration that I am describing, religious toleration is essentially similar to another case of toleration that I shall consider—toleration of prostitution or of the production, sale, and consumption of pornography. According to this tradition and unlike the case of some forms of liberalism, neither prostitution nor pornography can claim any protection as a matter of justice or rights—e.g., those devolving from freedom of speech in the latter case or from some notion of market freedom in the former. Within the tradition I am discussing, prostitution is a morally illicit use of the market and pornography a morally illicit use of speech or other forms of communication, and justice does not supply any right or liberty that could be invoked in support of moral evil. Again, however, prudential considerations pertaining to procuring a greater good or avoiding a worse evil lie at the heart of questions of toleration. With respect to prostitution and civil divorce, Häring writes,

> [S]ince the days of Augustine, many learned theologians have held that a legal regulation and with it also a species of public "toleration" of "legalized" prostitution under certain circumstances is lawful, provided it does not imply formal approval of this degrading vice and result in multiplication of sins. Similarly Christian politicians and jurists may cooperate in a legal regulation of civil divorce. But it is permitted only on condition that the circumstances do not favor a more rapid spread of the evil of divorce and the legal cooperation clearly does not imply moral approval of an evil which these leaders believe they cannot prevent by legislative action. Legal toleration or more accurately the hedging in of moral abuses, viewed in its totality, must serve and promote better morals.[44]

At least at the time he wrote *The Law of Christ*, Häring evi-

dently held that there were fewer compelling prudential reasons for tolerating traffic in pornography than for tolerating
civil divorce.[45] Whether this assumption holds true in, say, the
late twentieth-century United States is perhaps disputable. But
proponents of this viewpoint will attempt to interpret and define any relevant constitutional provisions in a manner that
permits the limitation of traffic in pornography to the degree
that prudential considerations permit. Feminist antipathy toward certain forms of pornography and also opposition origi-
nating from the "antichild-abuse movement," constitute part of
the complex totality of contingent social circumstances that
contemporary prudential calculation takes into account to determine the degree to and manner in which an intrinsic evil
should be tolerated. In other words, such a prudential view of
toleration and civility makes cooperation with favorable social
movements entirely feasible even in the presence of serious
disagreement about relevant deep principles.

It is important to emphasize the point that this traditional,
prudential conception of toleration and civility may often, in
the context of contemporary Western constitutional democracies,
have about the same 'output' with respect to concrete sociopolitical action as the competing, liberal conception of these social virtues. Where there are ambiguities, uncertainties, and
grey areas regarding the application of one conception, there
often will be analogous areas of disagreement in the application of the other conception. What is quite different are the
fundamental principles connected with the two conceptions,
particularly those principles pertaining to the relation between
the public, political sphere and issues of the "right" and
the "good." The liberal conception of toleration, which is ultimately grounded in a set of rights bestowed by an egalitarian political conception of justice, is committed to stopping
History at this particular sociopolitical juncture with a theory
that provides something approaching a categorical justification/
legitimation (and entrenchment) of what, from the more traditional perspective, represents only what is workable in a particular cultural, social, and political context. What is workable,
in this sense, often does not represent anything intrinsically
worthy of justification, legitimation, or entrenchment. That is,
the socially and politically workable often does consist of what
is morally categorical, in the sense of not being contingent on

a particular social/cultural/political context. Whereas political liberalism's desideratum of a political theory that is political and public turns out to be the demand for a moral justification of liberal institutions, principles, and attitudes that is "categorical" to the greatest possible extent, in the sense of resting only on such purportedly universal notions as rationality, reasonableness, equal respect, and Rawlsian primary goods.

Consequently, political liberalism's goal of stopping History by the rules—i.e., by the development of a public justifying/ legitimating theory that all rational and reasonable citizens should be able to endorse—is a goal that could be achieved only by writing off such non-liberal (but perfectly respectable) moral, philosophical, and religious traditions. We have found our way back to that now familiar problem of liberal political theory: the requirement of justifying the relatively less controversial in terms of the relatively more controversial. The relatively less controversial has taken shape within a particular context by means of the actual sociopolitical processes of compromise and search for modi vivendi. But the relatively more controversial, according to political liberalism, is a categorical, public justifying/legitimating theory. At the conclusion of the next and final chapter, I shall propose a minimalist and non-theoretical attitude toward democratic political process that has given up any attempt to "play by the rules" of such a supposed public but substantive justifying theory.

Notes

1. Herbert Marcuse, *Reason and Revolution: Hegel and the Rise of Social Theory* (Boston: Beacon Press, 1960), 344.

2. I realize, of course, that this characterization of the relation between liberal political theory and the results of supposedly contingent historical processes is controversial. And it certainly may not apply to all forms of liberal justifying/legitimating theory. However, a strong case may be made that, with respect to much 'classical modern' and contemporary liberal political theory, the following claim of George Parkin Grant is more-or-less correct: "English political philosophy has been little more than a praise of the fundamental lineaments of their own society, spiced by calls for particular reforms within those lineaments" (George Parkin Grant, *English-Speaking Justice* [Notre Dame, Ind.: University of Notre Dame Press, 1985], 51).

3. Thomas E. Hill, Jr., "The Stability Problem in *Political Liberalism*," *Pacific Philosophical Quarterly* 75, nos. 3 & 4 (September/December 1994): 336.

4. Ibid.

5. John Rawls, *Political Liberalism*, 142.

6. Ibid., 143.

7. Ibid., 142.

8. Hill, "The Stability Problem in *Political Liberalism*," 339.

9. Rawls, *Political Liberalism*, 140–141.

10. Brian Barry, "John Rawls and the Search for Stability," *Ethics* 105 (July, 1995): 913.

11. In *Political Liberalism* Rawls maintains that while the difference principle, *qua* principle of socioeconomic distribution, is a matter of "basic justice," it is not a "constitutional essential"—even though it falls within the scope of "political values" and is to be decided upon by "public reason." With respect to principles pertaining to social and economic inequalities, he says, "[t]hese matters are nearly always open to wide differences of reasonable opinion; they rest on complicated inferences and intuitive judgments that require us to assess complex social and economic information about topics poorly understood" (229).

12. Barry, "John Rawls and the Search for Stability," 913.

13. Hill, "The Stability Problem in *Political Liberalism*," 342.

14. Jeffrie G. Murphy makes a similar point about the role of consent in Kant's version of what I have termed the Rousseauian model of political legitimacy. He argues that what is essential for Kant is the 'reasonableness' of (possible) consent: "If reasonableness is accepted as a constraint on possible consent, however, then consent itself cannot play quite the foundational role that Kant envisions. It will at least share the foundational role with an account of reasonableness" ("Kant on Theory and Practice," in *Theory and Practice*, ed. Ian Shapiro and Judith DeCew [New York: New York University Press, 1965], 64–65.). I would add that it is really the relevant notion of reasonableness, not that of consent, that is doing the work and, thus, is 'foundational' here.

15. Rawls, *Political Liberalism*, 39–40.

16. Alasdair MacIntyre, *Whose Justice? Which Rationality?* (Notre Dame, Ind.: University of Notre Dame Press, 1988), 193.

17. Charles Larmore, *Patterns of Moral Complexity* (Cambridge: Cambridge University Press, 1987), 53.

18. Ibid., 53–54.

19. Ibid., 67.

20. Rawls, *Political Liberalism*, 50.

21. Gary C. Leedes, "Rawls's Excessively Secular Political Conception," *University of Richmond Law Review* 27, no.1083 (1994): 1104.

22. For Rawls's attempt to distinguish among "procedural neutrality," "neutrality of aim," and "neutrality of effect," see *Political Liberalism*, 190–195.

23. Lawrence B. Solum, "Inclusive Public Reason," *Pacific Philosophical Quarterly* 75, nos. 3 & 4 (September/December 1994): 218.

24. Ibid., 219.

25. Rawls, *Political Liberalism*, 217.

26. Solum, "Inclusive Public Reason," 223.

27. Rawls, *Political Liberalism*, 243, n. 32.

28. Peter de Marneffe, "Rawls's Idea of Public Reason," *Pacific Philosophical Quarterly* 75, nos. 3 & 4 (September/December 1994): 237.

29. Ronald Dworkin, "Why Liberals Should Care about Equality," in *A Matter of Principle* (Cambridge, Mass.: Harvard University Press, 1985), 205.

30. Ibid.

31. Margaret Moore, *Foundations of Liberalism* (Oxford: Clarendon Press, 1993), 177.

32. I thank Professor John Hittinger for emphasizing this point in his most perceptive and helpful comments on a draft of the manuscript of this book.

33. Plutarch, *De vitiosi pudore (On Compliancy)*, in *Plutarch's Moralia*, vol. 7, trans. Phillip H. de Lacy and Benedict Einarson, The Loeb Classical Library (Cambridge, Mass.: Harvard University Press, 1959), 529f.

34. Robertson Davies, *Fifth Business* (New York: Penguin Books, 1970), 48.

35. Rawls, *Political Liberalism*, 217.

36. Joseph Raz, *The Morality of Freedom* (Oxford: Clarendon Press, 1986), 401.

37. Ibid., 404.

38. Michael Davies, *The Second Vatican Council and Religious Liberty* (Long Prairie, Minn.: The Newman Press, 1992), 45.

39. Bernard Häring, *The Law of Christ*, vol. 2 (Westminster, Md.: The Newman Press, 1966), 430.

40. Ibid., 431.

41. St. Thomas Aquinas, *Summa Theologiae*, ed. P. Caramello (Turin and Rome: Marietti, 1952), II^a II^{ae} q. 10, a. 12.

42. Leo XIII, *Libertas praestantissimum*, translated as *On Human Liberty*, in *Papal Thought on the State*, ed. Gerald F. Yates (New York: Appleton-Century-Crofts, Inc., 1958), 49–50.

43. Ibid., 43.

44. Häring, *The Law of Christ*, vol. 1, 250.

45. Ibid., vol. 2, 492–93. Häring here maintains that "objectively speaking, evil books which have been borrowed are not to be returned to an owner who is in bad faith in his possession or use, except for a serious and good reason. There can be no claim in this instance that the right of property is violated, for in the eyes of God no one has a right to possess such thing" (493).

Chapter 4

Politics—Perfect and Imperfect

In his book *The Naked Public Square*, Richard John Neuhaus quotes the "memorable words" of G. K. Chesterton to the effect that "America is a nation with the soul of a church."[1] Because Neuhaus does not cite the source of the quotation and I have not been sufficiently motivated to attempt to locate it, I do not know whether the comment was intended seriously or ironically, with approval or disapprobation. I also am uncertain whether the judgment might ever plausibly have been said to be true. But two things seem to me to be fairly clear about the present American sociopolitical scene: The judgment is not now true, and many persons—including many political theorists—with quite disparate political allegiances would like to believe that it is true. I maintain that contemporary constitutional democracies (perhaps particularly the American one) are among the least psychic social institutions devised by humans: Thus, any attempt by political theory to co-opt such a supposed national soul is, at best, futile.

In effect, much of the tradition of contemporary political liberalism is committed to the discovery of such a soul and to the use of it as the foundational datum on which to construct its justifying/legitimating (and stabilizing/entrenching) theory. Rawls finds this political soul in his "political culture of a democratic society"; proponents of the ideal rational discourse model find it in the 'neutral ground' of rational dialogue together with a notion of "ideal conditions of rational dialogue" (whether understood "contextually," as does Larmore, or as something "transcendent and unconditioned," as Habermas gen-

123

erally does).[2] The hope of contemporary theorists of political liberalism has been to make such a political soul as 'public', secular, and neutral as possible—that is, to divorce it, so far as possible, from the concrete moral, religious, and philosophical commitments of individual citizens. I have thus far made the following claims about such a supposed liberal political soul or spirit. (a) It is commonly assumed that such a soul is the proper object of the ministrations of theorists of political liberalism, who should be able to represent this soul by means of a political theory or thick conception of distributive justice (such as Rawls's justice as fairness). (1) Such a theory is supposed to justify/legitimate some more-or-less determinate set of liberal institutions, principles, and attitudes (and, perhaps, stabilize/ entrench them). (2) The theory is also supposed to be 'projectible'—i.e., provide the theoretical means for addressing and resolving at least the basic questions of justice and constitutional issues that will confront a contemporary constitutional democracy. (b) The theoretical representation of political soul, within the liberal tradition, typically involves a combination of the attempt to justify actual social compromises and modi vivendi (and what is taken to be developing consensuses the vanguard of which are progressive popular movements) and the appeal to perfectionist considerations drawn from philosophical, religious, or moral doctrines. Common historical manifestations of such perfectionist considerations include the liberal (Rousseauian) conception of political legitimacy as deriving from the consent of suitably idealized agent-citizens, the political promotion of some concept of circumscribed autonomy (Kantian or otherwise) with respect to certain aspects of the lives of agent-citizens, and political focus on only selected aspects of agent-citizens' conceptions of the good. (c) Finally, I have characterized as misguided the idea that a political theory might justify or legitimate a set of liberal principles, institutions, and attitudes in a public manner—i.e., in a manner that might reasonably be expected to win the assent of all rational and reasonable citizens and thereby to stop History by stabilizing/ entrenching that political set-up. Such an idea entails the attempt to justify the less controversial (the concrete compromises, modi vivendi, acquiescences, and consensuses arrived at by historical social processes) by the more controversial (theory that will involve appeal to deep philosophical, moral, and religious principles).

True enough, the political soul that liberalism hopes to capture theoretically is a secularized, nonparticularized, Enlightened soul whose will is *la volonté générale* and whose motivation is the fulfillment of the impartial *amour de soi-même* common to all citizens. Nonetheless, for most theorists of political liberalism, there *is* such a spirit—one that is manifested, according to Rawls, in the "public political culture of a democratic society," which "comprises the political institutions of a constitutional regime and the public traditions of their interpretation (including those of the judiciary), as well as historic texts and documents that are common knowledge."[3] The phrases "public culture" and "public traditions" are particularly significant here. If one is looking for the soul or spirit of a contemporary constitutional democracy—or of a factitious person such as a nation, in general—it makes sense to attempt to locate it in a public culture or tradition. If one wishes to look beyond the concrete political practices, institutions, and attitudes of a particular society during some definite stretch of time, the conception of these phenomena as by-and-large manifestations of some shared public culture or tradition(s) is appealing.

Furthermore, if one is dealing with a contemporary constitutional democracy where such political arrangements are, supposedly, the result of democratic processes of compromise, acquiescence, and consensus and if one is engaged in the theoretical enterprise of attempting to justify/legitimate (and, perhaps, stabilize/entrench) these political arrangements, then the invocation of a shared political culture and traditions is even more useful. The placing of a culture/tradition as intermediary between concrete political data issuing from democratic processes and justifying theory can have the effect of softening the radically contingent character of the historiographical roots of liberal theory in the nitty-gritty politics of actual compromise and acquiescence. Rawls terms that radically contingent character "political in the wrong way." Achieving some fit between the concrete output of democratic political processes and liberal justifying theory may be a bit easier if the former can be filtered through a public culture/tradition, which can be invoked to block out the anomalous, introduce at least a degree of temporal coherence, and, in general, smooth out troublesome conceptual irregularities.

It is not surprising, then, that many of the skirmishes in the culture wars of the last decades of the twentieth century (at least in the United States) involve disagreements about what sociopolitical policies and attitudes best represent the supposed national soul and best conform to a supposed common political culture. The political culture discerned by liberal theorists such as Rawls is a rich, substantive one: According to Rawls, it is to be represented by and justified in terms of a full-fledged liberal political theory with elaborate (but controversial) normative consequences for the conduct of the nation's political business. Perhaps understandably, theorists of other persuasions have demurred with respect to the claim of liberal theory to represent the culture of contemporary constitutional democracies. Yet, a set of liberal institutions and political procedures, along with a good many substantive principles and attitudes, constitute *one* significant tradition in the contemporary Western world—a tradition that continues to enjoy a particular eminence in theoretical and academic circles. Consequently, much of the contemporary opposition to canonical theoretical liberalism has, in effect, been an attempt to implant certain distinctive sociopolitical concerns into an essentially liberal framework or to merge other intellectual and moral traditions with a selection of liberal values, attitudes, and principles. I shall next consider two illustrations of these intellectual maneuvers.

Lex Naturalis Redux:
Neo-Natural Law Theory and Liberalism

It is not unfair to say that the "wider" (non-Catholic) intellectual community has long regarded the natural-law tradition in ethics and political theory as well as in theology as a fundamentally sectarian business, without much to offer to that wider community nor much to contribute to the public discussion of moral and sociopolitical issues in contemporary liberal constitutional democracies. Recently, a group of theorists, including Joseph Boyle, John Finnis, Robert George, and Germain Grisez have attempted to introduce a reconceptualized natural-law theory into the public discussion of fundamental and not-so-fundamental moral and sociopolitical issues. Although deep commitment to the Catholic faith is common to this group, their neo-natural law theory may be represented as an attempt to "unbaptize" the theory of natural law and, thus, to bring it into dialogue with other prominent and usually secular contemporary moral and sociopolitical traditions—preeminently varieties of liberalism. The spirit of much of this work, in other words, is that of critical and discerning aggiornamento and rapprochement with the world—which often appears to be primarily the world of liberal sociopolitical theorists. In the words of Robert George,

> [I]t remains true that the natural law tradition has been slow to appreciate the insights of liberalism when it comes to basic civil liberties such as freedom of religion, speech, press, assembly, and the right to privacy. Moreover, it would be unjust to suggest that, since many natural law theorists and other critics of liberalism have now taken these insights on board, the achievements of liberalism are entirely in the past. Although I shall have critical things to say in this book about leading contemporary liberal philosophers, I also believe that work being done by many of these thinkers contains much that is true and important concerning individual freedom and the limits of law.[4]

Echoing George, I hold that there is "much that is true and important," and much that deserves further serious consideration, in the work of the neo-natural law theorists. Indeed, I typically find myself in agreement with their particular and midlevel ethical and sociopolitical claims. In the present section, however, I am concerned with the nature and consequences of neo-natural law theory's accommodations with liberalism and, in particular, with the question of whether neo-natural law theorists see themselves as presenting a justifying/legitimating political theory that, while in competition with justifying/legitimating theories of political liberalism, is supposed to be public and political in the manner of such theories. I should make clear that the emphasis of my discussion is not meant to imply that the intention of the neo-natural law theorists whom I discuss is to effect some rapprochement with theoretical liberalism, as opposed to search for the truth. Even less do I question the seriousness of the religious commitments of these

theorists. Yet, it seems that a noteworthy feature of this newly forming tradition is its search for a 'nonpartisan' stance with respect to the construction of a justifying/legitimating political theory. This obviously is a desideratum also shared by most theoretical versions of political liberalism.

As we saw in the first chapter, religious fragmentation, the potential for civil discord and persecution resulting from religious differences, and the practical necessity of constructing at least a tolerant modus vivendi in contexts of religious pluralism loom large in liberalism's own favored historiography. From that historiographical perspective, religious conviction sometimes involves passionate responses that are not carefully reasoned or considered and tends to be regarded as an especially divisive factor with respect to civic cooperation and the formation of social consensus. David Hume, with his customary irony and hyperbole, expresses this view of the relatively greater "danger" of religious, as compared to philosophical, belief:

> For as superstition [i.e., religion, according to Hume's frequent usage] arises naturally and easily from the popular opinions of mankind, it seizes more strongly on the mind, and is often able to disturb us in the conduct of our lives and actions. Philosophy on the contrary, if just, can present us only with mild and moderate sentiments; and if false and extravagant, its opinions are merely the objects of a cold and general speculation, and seldom go so far as to interrupt the course of our natural propensities . . . Generally speaking, the errors in religion are dangerous; those in philosophy only ridiculous.[5]

Of course, the "errors in religion" that Hume has in mind are precisely those convictions or practices that might threaten secular, sociopolitical irenicism or deflect persons from what he regards as the paths of natural virtue. With a conception of differences in religious belief as an especially troublesome source of social discord, it makes sense to eschew the sectarian in the development of a theory about the proper basis, nature, and justification of political prescriptions and proscriptions.

Although contemporary theorists of neo-natural law certainly do not share such suspicion or contempt of religion, they have generally been concerned to eliminate any sectarian odor from the foundations of their theory of natural law—in particular, from their formulation of a concept of the common good (*bonum commune*) to which law and the entire mechanism of political institutions, principles, and practices are ordered. In view of the very common liberal Enlightenment conception of religious conviction as a uniquely potent source of social/civic mischief, it may seem to make considerable sense to appeal to as secular a conception of the *bonum commune* as possible if one is attempting to enter into dialogue with proponents of contemporary liberal theories of sociopolitical morality.

Neo-natural law theorists have found grounds for this tactic in the origins of the Thomistic tradition of natural law. St. Thomas certainly holds that there are important distinctions between nature and grace, between our natural end and our supernatural end, between practical reason and faith, and between *lex naturalis* (natural law) and *lex divina* (divine law). As he puts it,

> [I]f man were ordained only to so great an end as not to surpass that proportionate to the natural human faculty, there would be no need for man to have any direction on the part of reason beyond natural law and positive human law, which is derived from it. But since man is ordained to the end of eternal beatitude, which exceeds what is proportionate to the natural human faculty, as stated above, it was therefore necessary that, in addition to natural and human law, he should be directed to his own end by divinely given law.[6]

Perhaps it is the case, then, that the theory of natural law can accommodate a secular conception of the human good, from which principles of morality, including political morality, can be derived that will be morally binding on all rational persons as such and that can be kept separate from sectarian issues of revelation, faith, and the hermeneutics of the *lex divina*.

In his *Natural Law and Natural Rights* John Finnis, according to his own characterization, "offers a rather elaborate sketch of a theory of natural law without needing to advert to the question of God's existence or nature or will," while commenting that

> the fact that natural law can be understood, assented to, applied, and reflectively analysed without adverting to the question of the

existence of God does not of itself entail either (i) that no further explanation is required for the fact that there are objective standards of good and bad and principles of reasonableness (right and wrong), or (ii) that no such explanation is available, or (iii) that the existence of God is not that explanation.[7]

As we have seen, Rawls also seeks a theory of public, political morality that is based on the sort of rationality and reasonableness captured in his concept of public reason. This public reason, according to Rawls's conception of it, does not need to advert to any particular comprehensive conception of the good (even any reasonable one), which will contain its own partisan or sectarian philosophical, moral, or religious principles. A liberal justifying/legitimating political theory—produced, defended, and preserved by Rawlsian rationality and reasonableness—would thus be a freestanding module capable of being incorporated, in a variety of different ways, into at least the reasonable comprehensive conceptions of the good. Analogously, neo-natural law theorists of the school of Grisez, Finnis, and George seek a theory of morality (including public morality) based on a thicker conception of practical rationality. While this practical rationality *does* advert to the components of a substantive but multifaceted conception of the objective human good, it need not presuppose any partisan or sectarian metaphysical or theological context into which practical reason, according to this conception, must be fitted. A neo-natural law moral theory—produced, defended, and preserved by practical reason—apparently would also be a freestanding module capable of being incorporated into a variety of different theological and metaphysical contexts.

Grisez and Finnis begin with the first principle of the natural law: "[G]ood is to be done and pursued and evil avoided" (*"[B]onum est faciendum et prosequendeum, et malum vitandum"*).[8] In the words of Russell Hittinger, this first principle of practical reason (Fppr)

necessarily spawns a plurality of directives or "practical principles." There are as many practical principles as there are values grasped in the mode of "ends-to-be-pursued" by action. Each of the practical principles is a specification of the general Fppr formula. In the older scholastic parlance, [Grisez] notes, these were known as the "primary precepts" of natural law.[9]

In other words, the first specification of the Fppr involves the determination of a list of "basic forms of good grasped by practical understanding."[10] Although the items in the list specify, in a general way, "what is good for human beings with the nature they have,"[11] the list is not constituted by empirical, psychological or sociological research, yielding some generalizations about what all (mentally competent, mature, etc.) persons desire or even, on reflection, admit to be good. Nor is the list the product of metaphysical or theological theory, which might postulate a teleological, perhaps multifaceted, characterization of human nature along the lines of the MacIntyre's factual/normativeman-as-he-could-be-if-he-realised-his-essential-nature. "Rather," says Finnis, "by a simple act of non-inferential understanding one grasps that the object of the inclination which one experiences is an instance of a general form of good, for oneself (and others like one)."[12]

Intra- and cross-cultural nose-counting, the imaginative consideration of possible instantiations of the human good are, ultimately, only aids and stimuli to these "simple act[s] of non-inferential [practical] understanding." The "basic forms of good for us" according to Finnis (Grisez' list differs slightly[13]) are life, knowledge, play, aesthetic experience, sociability (friendship), practical reasonableness, and religion.[14] Attributing his view to St. Thomas, Finnis glosses the self-evident and indemonstrable character that he ascribes to such a list of primary precepts by the comment that

> [i]t amounts to no more than saying that any sane person is capable of seeing that life, knowledge, fellowship, offspring, and a few other such basic aspects of human existence are, as such, good, i.e. worth having, leaving to one side all particular predicaments and implications, all assessments of relative importance, all moral demands, and in short, all questions of whether and how one is to devote oneself to these goods.[15]

Finnis, along with Grisez et al., maintain that these forms of human good initially (*qua* specifications of the Fppr) present themselves as independent and 'coordinate', in the sense of being irreducible and not characterized by any hierarchy of subordination with respect to relative value.

It is important to note that neo-natural law theory, in the

style of Grisez and Finnis, regards this 'first stage' of development, the Fppr and specification of "the List," as 'pre-moral':

> By disclosing a horizon of attractive possibilities for us, our grasp
> of the basic values thus creates, not answers, the problem for in-
> telligent decision: What is to be done? What may be left undone?
> What is not to be done? . . .
>   The principles that express the general ends of human life do
> not acquire what would nowadays be called a 'moral' force until
> they are brought to bear upon definite ranges of project, disposi-
> tion, or action, or upon particular projects, dispositions, or actions.
> How they are thus to be brought to bear *is* the problem for prac-
> tical reasonableness. 'Ethics', as classically conceived, is simply a
> recollectively and/or prospectively reflective expression of this
> problem and of the general lines of solutions which have been
> thought reasonable.[16]

The "good" of practical reasonableness, then, is the basis
of moral obligation. As is the case with respect to Kantian
moral theory and most liberal theories of political morality,
neo-natural law theory locates morality in the procedures or
manner in which human goods are to be pursued. But, partly
because neo-natural law theory proposes a determinate, objective account of the forms of human good, it presents a much
less formal and thin account of morality as procedural.

In his critical account of neo-natural law theory, Hittinger
usefully calls attention to the fact that the neo-natural law theory's first principle of morality (Fpm)—*qua* imperative pertaining to procedure for realizing the human good—is schematic
in the same way as is the Fppr—*qua* imperative pertaining to
the content of the human good. Grisez characterizes the Fpm
as follows: "In voluntarily acting for human goods and avoiding what is opposed to them, one ought to choose and otherwise will those and only those possibilities whose willing is
compatible with a will toward integral human fulfillment."[17]
Finnis speaks here of the imperative of "committing oneself to
a rational plan of life."[18] But such a plan will be shaped, in
terms of its end, by the forms of human good; morality (including political morality) is not to be thought of a set of *external* procedural directives and constraints applied to an
otherwise *arbitrary* life plan or conception of the good.

The next level of specification of the Fpm leads to a "second List" of procedural directives and principles. In the case of Finnis: (1) there is a general requirement of a "rational plan of life," which implies that the forms of human good be "realizable only by one who intelligently directs, focuses, and controls his urges, inclinations, and impulses" (103). (2) "Next, there must be no leaving out of account, or arbitrary discounting or exaggeration, of any of the basic human values" (105). (3) The third principle, related to the modern notion of the universalizability of moral judgments and preferences, proscribes "arbitrary preferences among persons" (106–109). (4) The fourth principle prescribes "a certain detachment from all the specific and limited projects which one undertakes": It proscribes the development of an attitude that "one's life is drained of meaning" in the event of failure of such projects, an attitude that "irrationally devalues and treats as meaningless the basic good of authentic and reasonable determination" (110). (5) The fifth principle "is simply the requirement that having made one's general commitments one must not abandon them lightly (for to do so would mean, in the extreme cases, that one would fail ever to really participate in any of the basic values)" (110). (6) The sixth principle is the "requirement that one bring about good in the world (in one's own life and the lives of others) by actions that are efficient for their (reasonable) purpose(s)" (111). (7) Finally, the seventh principle is important for the derivation of some of the most distinctive and controversial moral positions of the neo-natural law theorists and also, according to Finnis, for the derivation of the "strict inviolability of basic human rights" (121). Although it can be expressed in multiple forms, it is in essence a prescription of "respect for every basic value in every act" (118–25). In the case of Grisez (who, again, has a slightly different "second List"), this imperative is expressed as follows: "One should not be moved by a stronger desire for one instance of an intelligible good to act for it by choosing to destroy, damage, or impede some other instance of an intelligible good."[19]

It is clear that even the basic theoretical lineaments of neo-natural law theory deserve further exegesis. But I hope that the preceding account is sufficient to render the following discussion intelligible for readers who may not be familiar with this relatively new movement. Various aspects of neo-natural law theory (as opposed to more traditional natural law theory or what I call "paleo-natural law theory") are obviously more congenial to the Enlightenment, liberal *Weltanschauung*. The Grisez-Finnis-George style of neo-natural law theory emphasizes the multifaceted character of the human good and the "inexhaustibly many . . . [morally acceptable] life-plans that differing individuals may choose"[20] by application of their faculty of practical rationality or reasonableness. The idea of the *homo faber sui* (the self-constructing human) or (in Finnis's words), the "fundamental task of practical reasonableness [as] self-constitution or self-possession,"[21] is a pervasive Enlightenment (and post-Enlightenment) trope that, in various forms, has found its way into liberal sociopolitical thought. It has evidently found its way into neo-natural law theory as well. But, in neo-natural law theory, the limits of self-construction are constituted not exclusively by a Rawlsian (or Kantian) conception of the moral "right" that is separable from the human "good" but by substantive forms of that human good as well. Emphasis on autonomous self-construction is, naturally enough, accompanied by an attempt to construct a "principled defense" of liberal freedoms. Thus, a goal of Robert George is to show that neo-natural law theory provides a conceptual framework "which articulates a legitimate realm for morals legislation and still permits a desirable diversity of ways of life and provides principled grounds for respecting and protecting basic civil liberties such as freedom of religion, speech, press, and assembly, and a right to privacy."[22]

It seems, however, that *the* salient theoretical feature of neo-natural law theory is its attempt to liberate the moral and, hence, the political theory of natural law from any supposed metaphysical or theological foundation. In justifying this theoretical stance, Grisez, Finnis, et al., appeal to the dictum of classical Modern moral philosophy forbidding the derivation of value from fact, an 'ought' from an 'is'. Theological or metaphysical claims about a teleologically structured natural world, the manifestation of the Divine providence that is St. Thomas's *lex aeterna* (eternal law), and the consequent natural human ends against which empirical human inclinations, desires, and wants can be measured, all have to do with the realm of purported fact. If we are to avoid the 'fallacy' of inferring an 'ought' from an 'is', we must conceive the first precepts of natural law as freestanding principles of practical rationality and avoid the temptation to think of them as somehow conditional on factual claims about what is and what is not natural with respect to human inclinations and the use of human faculties.

It has sometimes been supposed that the stricture against inference of value from fact is a straightforward matter of logic. It is not. It is indeed true that, in the syllogistic and in the standard contemporary formulations of the predicate calculus, one usually needs an 'ought' in at least one of the premises of an argument that is valid in the lower predicate calculus (or a syllogistically-valid argument) to get an 'ought' in the conclusion.[23] But this is a technical matter of quite limited conceptual import. Contemporary logic has the resources to supply the requisite sorts of premise or the requisite rules of inference for deriving normative or evaluative conclusions from factual premises in the substantive sense in which philosophers might be concerned with the connection or lack of connection between fact and value. Of course, contemporary logic also has the resources for insuring that such inferences will be blocked, if that is what is required of it by metaphysical/moral theory.

David Hume is a particularly prominent classical Modern proponent of a rigid separation between 'is' and 'ought'. This doctrine is employed by him in support of a very restricted conception of reason or the "understanding" as a theoretical (and essentially passive) faculty for ascertaining "an agreement or disagreement either to *real* relations of ideas, or to *real* existence and matter of fact."[24] *Action*, for Hume, must find its "springs" in the passions. And, says Hume, "[w]here a passion is neither founded on false suppositions, nor chuses means insufficient for the end, the understanding can neither justify nor condemn it. 'Tis not contrary to reason to prefer the destruction of the world to the scratching of my finger."[25]

St. Thomas's location of natural law and the normative employment of practical reason within the 'factual' context of the teleology of the *lex aeterna* is a substantive theoretical claim—one open to question, no doubt, but not an instance of a simple logical fallacy:

> [I]t is manifest that all things participate to a degree in the eternal law, insofar, indeed, from its imprint they have their inclinations to their proper acts and ends. Among the rest, however, the ra-

tional creature is subject to divine providence in a distinctive, more excellent manner, insofar as it becomes a participant in providence by being provident for itself and for others. Whence it participates in itself in the eternal reason, through which it has a natural inclination to its own due (*debitum*) act and end. And such participation of the eternal law in the rational creature is called natural law.[26]

Finnis argues that this theological/metaphysical contextualization of natural law and practical reason is a consequence of the fact that "Aquinas himself was a writer not on ethics alone but on the whole of theology. He was keen to show the relationship between his ethics of natural law and his general theory of metaphysics and the world-order."[27] He further claims, that even for St. Thomas, natural-law ethics is freestanding, correctly pointing out that Aquinas holds that the first principles of natural law are indemonstrable and *nota per se* (known through themselves).

More controversially, Finnis claims that St. Thomas does not really employ his theological/metaphysical teleology, *qua* matter of theoretical or 'speculative' fact, in the derivation of the midlevel and particular moral obligations imposed by practical reason, *qua* matter of value: "[F]or Aquinas, the way to discover what is morally right (virtue) and wrong (vice) is to ask, not what is in accordance with human nature, but what is reasonable."[28] Although subtle interpretive and philosophical issues are involved, it seems that St. Thomas typically does not see any difference, and certainly no opposition, between "what is accordance with human nature" and "what is reasonable." And he *does* sometimes argue for particular moral positions in terms of conformity with nature. To take but one example, Aquinas takes a strong, almost rigorist, position against lying: Even "jocular" and "officious" morally well-intentioned lies are evil (although not always mortal sins):

> [A] lie is evil with respect to its genus (*ex genere*). It is an act categorized by inappropriate ('undue': *indebitum*) matter: for since words are naturally signs of meanings, it is unnatural and inappropriate (*innaturale est et indubitum*) that anyone should signify by word that which he does not have in mind.[29]

It seems clear that St. Thomas is relying on the premise that speech or language, *ex genere* and in its assertoric mode, is ordered by God's providential *lex aeterna* and the human rational participation in that law, i.e., *lex naturalis*, toward the end of truth (and, ultimately the Truth). Thus, "what is properly evil *ex genere* can in no way be good and licit."[30] I am not claiming that it would be impossible to come to the same conclusion with respect to lying by the methods of argument of the neo-natural law theorists, eschewing any appeal to theistic teleology. But I am not convinced that any such argument would be more persuasive (even to the unchurched) than that of Aquinas.

It is most plausible to view Aquinas's *lex aeterna* as embodying a theistic world view in which natural law arguments 'make sense'—not necessarily as supplying further theological/metaphysical *premises* from which the first principles of natural law, and subsequent midlevel and particular conclusions of natural law, are deductively inferred. Traditional or paleo-natural law theory also makes use of a *tradition* of interpretation or application that contains principles such as that employed by St. Thomas in deriving his strictures against any form of lying: That is, for an action to be good, all its causes (including the generic or 'material' cause—the *sort* of action that it is) must concur in rectitude.[31] Neo-natural law theory has not been around sufficiently long to have built up an altogether adequate set of such canons or traditions of interpretation/application. Without them, neo-natural law arguments for many midlevel and particular moral conclusions will be open to dispute, even within the general conceptual framework of the theory itself. For example, there is a considerable conceptual distance between recognition of life as a basic form of good (even "life" in the sense that includes "procreation") and the conclusion of Finnis (and Grisez) that contraception is morally illicit. Part of what fills in the gap is not a moral principle at all but a factual (metaphysical?) claim that contraception is instantiated in acts *distinct* from any acts of sexual behavior to which contraception may be connected. In the words of Finnis,

[b]eing thus a distinct chosen act, contraception is defined by its intention, which simply is that a prospective new human life not begin. Choosing to contracept is simply contralife, whatever else can be said, and rightly said, about the morally significant features of the sexual act performed *as* contracepted.[32]

As a distinct act essentially defined by a contralife intention, a contraceptive act clearly contradicts Finnis's "first formulation" of his "seventh requirement of practical reasonableness": "one should not choose to do any act which *of itself does nothing but* damage or impede a realization or participation of any one or more of the basic forms of human good."[33] As much as I agree with Finnis concerning the moral character of contraception, it seems likely that this "distinct act" assumption might well be one link in the chain between good of life and immorality of contraception that would be questioned by someone outside the natural law tradition who is sympathetic with the general outline of neo-natural law theory's characterization of forms of human good but who is unsympathetic with any moral proscriptions against contraception.

To return to my principal concern with neo-natural law theory, i.e., the nature of its accommodations with liberalism and its conception of the sociopolitical role of its moral theory, how are we to assess it? No doubt most neo-natural law theorists would maintain that their primary intention is to construct the true (or most plausibly true) moral theory while working within the general tradition of natural law theory. Judgments concerning their success in this undertaking depend, I believe, on one's conception of the nature and function of the moral theory (with sociopolitical ramifications) that they have constructed. Most advocates of most moral theories, including neo-natural law theorists, are aiming at moral truth. Their theory has the primary function of trying to capture and represent that truth, and insofar as it succeeds in doing so, its prescriptions and proscriptions are taken to have an objective and public morally obligatory character. Political liberalism, however, generally aspires to a political justifying/legitimating theory that is 'public' in an additional and different sense. Such a theory *is itself* regarded as a proper object of public consensus, usually an idealized public consensus limited to rational and reasonable citizens of good will (who, insofar as they are reasonable in the Rawlsian sense, will separate the issue of their endorsement of such a theory from partisan commitments of a religious, philosophical, or private moral nature).

It is not clear whether neo-natural law theorists share the liberal aspiration for a theory that is objective and public in this strong sense. Irrespective of the intentions of theorists such as Grisez and Finnis, their attempt to decontextualize natural law with respect to a metaphysical or religious framework has the appearance of a liberal enterprise: an attempt to develop a more 'neutral' moral (and sociopolitical) theory in the spirit of consensus-formation. To reiterate my earlier claim, this decontextualization cannot be justified simply as a logical matter of avoiding some supposed "naturalistic fallacy" or of taking care not to derive an 'ought' from an 'is'. There is a real choice to be made in the matter, one that evidently may be justified in some manner—either theoretically or practically. I do not propose to enter further into the theoretical issues. In my view, neo-natural law theory has much to offer as a theory of objective morality, but one that is 'partisan' in the following sense: It derives from an intellectual (religious, philosophical, moral) tradition not shared by everyone in contemporary liberal democracies. And it seems most plausible to expect that many citizens from such democracies would repudiate it after serious consideration—but not necessarily because of any failure of rationality or reasonableness on their part. As a practical matter, I suspect that neo-natural law theory will not enjoy appreciably more success at theoretical consensus-building than paleo-natural law theory.

Although the fact that neo-natural law theory aims to prescind from any metaphysical or theological foundation might seem to contribute to its consensual status, there is a price to be paid. Its first precepts, the basic forms of human good, are left in a free-floating or, to use a different metaphor, dangling position. In this respect, neo-natural law theory's list of 'basic forms of the good' are much like the lists of 'basic liberties' of many contemporary liberal theories: having been, in the words of J. G. Murphy, "cut off from [their] traditional [metaphysical or theological] roots," such claims may seem to "hang in mid-air."[34] In other words, despite the disavowal of such a doctrine by Finnis and other neo-natural law theorists,[35] their assertions concerning forms of the human good may seem to amount to a form of intuitionism. Hittinger asks whether "we" (neo-natural law theorists) are "locked into an intuitive realm that cannot be further discussed or articulated"[36] and further comments:

> Intuitionism does not necessarily imply any theistic or supernatural content; but, once again, to the extent that it supplies the foun-

dational evidence for principles and norms, intuitionism differs from fideism only by denomination. Fideism can be defined as the intuition of revealed or supernatural data which are purported to be foundational.[37]

Intuitions notoriously differ and, as contemporary liberal theorists have emphasized, this is particularly true with respect to moral and sociopolitical issues within the context of 'pluralistic' contemporary liberal democracies. Paleo-natural law theory (and the Judaeo-Christian-Islamic tradition, in general) have something to say about this matter in the form of the doctrine of the Fall, Original Sin, and the corruption of the human faculties of intellect, will, and affect (cf. St. Thomas on the 'law of the fomes', *Summa Theologiae*, I^a II^{ae}, q. 91, a. 6). Neo-natural law theorists can, if they wish, appeal to revelation to explain the empirical diversity of moral judgments. They can also appeal to anthropological, psychological, or sociological 'empirical' claims to attempt to substantiate claims about essential agreement concerning fundamental issues of value. But, in doing so, in introducing issues of fact as opposed to issues of value, they are no longer arguing strictly in terms of natural law and are no longer confining themselves strictly to issues of practical rationality, according to their own conceptions of natural law and of practical rationality. That is, they have thus abandoned a strictly *moral* perspective, according to their own conception of it.

Consequently, in terms of developing a version of natural law theory upon which a theoretical consensus could be constructed, neo-natural law theory's prospects are no better than the paleo version. Either neo-natural lawyers are left with assertions (e.g., about the distinctive forms of human goodness) which look like claims of moral intuition and which, while eminently disputable in the intellectual milieu of contemporary liberal democracies, cannot be "further discussed or articulated" *within neo-natural law theory itself*. Or they can be "further discussed and articulated" only from the perspective of some religious, philosophical, or anthropological/sociological theory that neo-natural law theorists themselves seem to believe to be controversial and not plausible material for the formation of theoretical consensus.

Furthermore, the midlevel and determinate conclusions that

neo-natural law theorists actually have drawn from their theory, however morally correct these conclusions may be, militate against its acceptability as a theory that is 'public' in the sense of a consensus-theory. For example, conclusions concerning the immorality of contraception and homosexuality (as well as abortion) certainly seem to be inconsistent with what are— or what are commonly understood to be—liberal attitudes and values. And Robert George's arguments for the principled moral acceptability (although not necessarily pragmatic desirability) of various forms of 'legislation of morality' represent a point of view that seems unlikely to be accepted, in principle, by liberals on the basis of neo-natural law first principles. Especially with respect to moral or sociopolitical justifying/legitimating theory, one person's *modus ponens* is another's *modus tollens*. That is, let us suppose that neo-natural law theorists can produce cogent arguments for such conclusions. That very fact may well lead those who, on the basis of *other* considerations, do not sympathize with those conclusions to repudiate the underlying theoretical framework from which the controversial conclusions were 'derived'.

I believe, then, that neo-natural law theory must be judged on its philosophical, moral, and religious cogency: it is not a very plausible candidate for a 'public', consensual, sociopolitical theory that is supposed to satisfy the justifying/ legitimating function for contemporary Western liberal constitutional polity, i.e., the sort of public function that political liberalism envisions for such a theory. Of course, as I have mentioned, it is far from clear that neo-natural law theorists envision such a role for their own theory. However, one area in which neo-natural law theory does seem to aim for something like a public theoretical consensus is that of religion, considered as a basic form of human good.

Religion as a Basic Form of Human Good?

One of the basic forms of human good is designated by Finnis as 'religion' (with scare quotes). By this term Finnis means, primarily, attention to the question of whether it is perhaps the case that human freedom, in which one rises above the determinism of instinct and impulse to an intelligent grasp of worthwhile forms of good, and through which one shapes and masters one's environment but also one's character, is itself somehow subordinate to something which makes that human freedom, human intelligence, and human mastery possible (not just 'originally' but from moment to moment) and which is free, intelligent, and sovereign in a way (and over a range) no human being can be?[38]

Finnis admits that "there are, always, those who doubt or deny that the universal order-of-things has any origin beyond the 'origins' known to the natural sciences, and who answer [the preceding question] negatively" (89). But, he suggests, it is nonetheless "peculiarly important to have thought reasonably and (where possible) correctly about these questions of the origins of cosmic order and of human freedom and reason— whatever the answer to those questions turns out to be, and even if the answers have to be agnostic or negative" (89). The existence of such 'eternal' questions about a transcendent order behind the cosmos and behind human reason, freedom, and responsibility—whatever the shape of the answer one works out for oneself to such questions—is, claims Finnis, "more important for us than the ubiquity of religious concerns, in all human cultures" (90). It is here that Finnis locates the basis of the intelligible human good of 'religion'. In a similar vein, Robert George writes that

[i]rrespective of whether unaided reason can conclude on the basis of valid argument that God exists—indeed, even if it turns out that God does not exist—there is an important sense in which religion is a basic human good, and intrinsic and irreducible aspect of the well-being and flourishing of human persons. Religion is a basic human good if it provides an ultimate intelligible reason for action. But agnostics and even atheists can easily grasp the intelligible point of considering whether there is some ultimate, more-than-human source of meaning and value, of enquiring as best one can into the truth of the matter, and of ordering one's life on the basis of one's best judgment. Doing that is participating in the good of religion. Just as one has *reason* . . . to pursue knowledge, enter into friendships and other forms of community, strive for personal integrity, develop one's skills and realize one's talents, one also has reason, without appeal to ulterior reasons, to ascer-

tain the truth about ultimate or divine reality and, if possible, to establish harmony and enter into communion with the ultimate source(s) of meaning and value.[39]

According to this account, the value of religion as a basic form of human good is located in the enterprise of inquiry into an ultimate ground of "meaning and value," the pursuit of this inquiry to some sort of conclusion (perhaps a tentative or agnostic one), and the ordering of one's life-plan in conformity with this resolution. It appears that other 'communitarian' or cultic aspects of religiosity, e.g., offering sacrifice, worship, adoration, engaging in altruistic works, adopting a particular moral perspective and attempting to live in conformity with it, occupy a subsidiary place in neo-natural law theory's conception of the good of 'religion'.

Indeed, the neo-natural law conception of religion seems to be quite rationalistic. In view of this fact, it is perhaps surprising that Grisez, Finnis, and George all distinguish the good of 'religion' or holiness (as a basic form of human good) from the good of knowledge. A principal reason for the distinction between the good of religion and that of knowledge in neo-natural law theory must be a characteristic modern conception about religiosity or the 'religious impulse' that leads human beings to posit the question about a transcendent, ultimate source of meaning and value. According to this conception, the answer to this question is a private, individual 'framework decision' about one's life-plan—something along the lines of a 'Fundamental Option'.[40] According to neo-natural law theory, one's response to this 'Fundamental Option' is not really a matter of practical reason. That is, according to neo-natural lawyers, an objective fundamental morality can be preserved irrespective of the way one responds to the 'Fundamental Option'—although they are willing to allow that, from the 'perspective of faith', one's moral understanding can be strengthened and deepened.[41]

But it is not clear that neo-natural law theorists believe that one's response to the 'Fundamental Option'—how one addresses and answers the question of a transcendent, ultimate source of meaning and value—is really a matter of theoretical or 'speculative' reason either. Finnis, for example, thinks that speculative reason, unaided by faith or revelation, may perhaps allow us to derive the existence of a state of affairs (which he calls

"D"), viz., "a state of affairs which exists simply by being what
it is, and which is required for the existing of any other state
of affairs (including the state of affairs: D's causing all caused
states of affairs)."[42] But he is evidently doubtful that 'unaided
reason' could purchase us more knowledge about the properties of D, properties that have generally been considered essential to the Christian (or Judaic, or Islamic) conceptions of D
qua God. Here, by the way, is another reason for at least some
neo-natural law theorists to eschew the traditional, paleo-
theistic/metaphysical contextualization of natural law. If it is
questionable whether 'unaided reason' could produce cogent arguments for D's possessing sufficient properties (e.g., being a
provident *orderer* or law giver) to underwrite a (Thomistic) theistic teleology, perhaps one could preserve such a theistic/
metaphysical contextualization for the theory of natural law
only by appeal to revelation. And would not that be obviously
'sectarian'? There is some reason to accept Hittinger's claim
(concerning Grisez but also applying to Finnis) that "[h]is criticism of the older theory's heavy-handed emphasis on speculative reason also inclined him to the view that speculative
reason, including its metaphysical mode, is able to affirm little, if anything, about God as an end of human striving."[43]

Thus, practical reason is not, as a matter of principle (keeping 'ought' separate from 'is' and keeping the foundations of
morality as free as possible from sectarianism), able to contribute to resolution of the 'Fundamental Option' concerning a transcendent source of meaning and value. And theoretical or
speculative reason is an apparently doubtful and uncertain aid
in this regard. Consequently, it is not so difficult to understand
why neo-natural law theorists, while conceiving the good of
religion in intellectualist terms, yet distinguish it as a basic form
of human good distinct from knowledge. Because it seems plausible that each person must address the Fundamental Option
for herself or himself, the neo-natural law *foundation* of religiosity as a form of human good—if not all the possible forms of
expression of the religious impulse—is a quite private, individual matter. As George puts it,

> no one can search for religious truth, hold religious beliefs, or act
> on them authentically, for someone else. Searching, believing, and
> striving for authenticity are interior acts of individual human be-

ings. As interior acts, they cannot be compelled. If they are not freely done, they are not done at all.[44]

As a consequence of his and the general neo-natural law conception of the good of religion, irrespective of the choice one ends up making in response to the 'Fundamental Option', George adopts a conception of the 'liberty of conscience' that is virtually identical to the liberal conception:

> For the sake of religion, then, considered as a value that practical reason can identify as an intrinsic aspect of the integral good of all human beings, government may never legitimately coerce religious belief; nor may it require religious observance or practice, nor may it forbid them *for religious reasons*. (To that extent, freedom of religion *is* absolute.) Moreover, government, for the sake of the good of religion, should protect individuals and religious communities from others who would try to coerce them in religious matters *on the basis of theological objections to their beliefs and practices*.[45] (emphasis added)

George adds that "[b]ecause such a reason [i.e., support of the "value of religion"] can be defeated by other reasons, religious freedom is not an absolute. Clearly there are conclusive reasons to forbid human sacrifice or religiously motivated chattel slavery, for example, and even, perhaps, to prohibit the use of dangerous drugs in bona fide religious worship."[46]

As the italicized phrases in the preceding quotation indicate, George repudiates any religious or theological grounds as legitimate reasons for political 'interference' with religious liberty or 'freedom of conscience'. However, the sort of perfectionist argument that he invokes in behalf of both political religious liberty and political religious neutrality, relying as it does on his (and Grisez's and Finnis's) conception of the good of 'generic' religion, may require him to go further. It seems reasonable to suppose that it would be legitimate, in principle, for government to support and further the good of religion. But this support would have to be support for religion in general, support for each person's individual attempt to wrestle with the 'Fundamental Option', or, in George's words, encouragement and support for "religious reflection, faith, and practice." Note that this is support for 'generic' religiosity, not for any particular religious bodies or traditions. Because appeal to any religious or theological reasons is ruled out for a basis of making political discriminations among such bodies or traditions, it seems that a political policy of strict neutrality is mandated. George does not indicate whether such neutrality, in pursuit of the good of religiosity, requires the government to give differential assistance in such a way that poorer or otherwise less advantaged religious bodies or traditions are assisted in obtaining "equal time," so to speak, in the noncoercive propagation of their particular perspective on the Fundamental Option.

In brief, because the neo-natural law conception of the basic good of religion eschews any religious or theological orientation, much the same sort of neutrality toward religious matters characteristic of both political and perfectionist liberalism is supported, on perfectionist grounds of furthering the good of 'generic' religion, by neo-natural law theorists. This position differs from what I call the traditional Roman Catholic view, dominant until the Second Vatican Council. This traditional Catholic view is succinctly presented by Michael Davies:

> The traditional Catholic teaching is that in religious matters:
>
> 1. No one must be forced to act against his conscience in private.
>
> 2. No one must be forced to act against his conscience in public.
>
> 3. No one must be prevented from acting in accordance with his conscience in private.
>
> 4. The right of acting in accordance with one's conscience in public can be restricted.
>
> Catholicism and Liberalism concur on all four points, but differ on the criteria for restricting the expression of private belief in the external public forum. As will be explained in subsequent chapters, Catholicism posits the public good as the limiting criterion, while Liberalism accepts public order as the only legitimate criterion for restraint.[47]

"Public order" is usually cashed out, within the liberal tradition, in terms of something like the harm principle: political interference with action *in foro externo* (in external behavior) in conformity with religious convictions is legitimate only if such religiously motivated behavior harms others, particularly in terms of violating what are taken to be the fundamental rights of others.[48] Because, according to the traditional Catholic view, the common good has a particular religious/theological dimension, certain sorts of political interference with religiously motivated behavior *in foro externo* (e.g., differentially supporting one religious tradition, placing some restrictions on the proselytizing of other traditions) may, in principle, be legitimate in pursuit of that common good. The traditional position holds that prudential considerations always weigh heavily with respect to such political actions and has generally maintained that, in religiously pluralistic contemporary constitutional democracies such as the United States, such prudential considerations would count decisively against most forms of differential support of particular religious traditions or bodies among those represented in the populace.

In some respects the neo-natural law position on religious liberty or freedom of conscience approaches nearer to a standard liberal position than does the position developed in the *Declaration on Religious Freedom (Dignitatis humanae)* of the Second Vatican Council. As is well known, *Dignitatis humanae* represents the resolution of a struggle between forces, led by Cardinal Ottaviani, favoring the Church's traditional, 'pragmatic' stance on religious liberty and forces, led by the American Jesuit theologian John Courtney Murray, favoring a more 'principled' endorsement of religious liberty. It is common opinion that Murray's faction largely prevailed, and there seems to be ample historical support for the contention of Michael Davies that "Father Murray was determined to ensure that Church teaching was brought into line with the American Constitution."[49] However, the document represents its doctrine as being continuous with and a legitimate and needed 'development' of the traditional doctrine, a viewpoint that is supportable but controversial. I emphasize that I am not competent to make any judgment concerning the magisterial status of the 'new' doctrine, the degree to which it is to be regarded as obliging assent on the part of Roman Catholics or whether it satisfies accepted canons of the 'development of doctrine.' My present interest in the doctrine of *Dignitatis humanae* is exclusively philosophical and historical.

Article 7 of the document discusses possible restrictions of religious freedom as a matter of protection from "possible abuses committed in the name of religious freedom":

However, this must not be done in an arbitrary manner or by the unfair practice of favoritism but in accordance with legal principles in conformity with the objective moral order. These principles are necessary for the effective protection of the rights of all citizens and for peaceful settlement of conflicts of rights. They are also necessary for an adequate protection of the just public peace which is to be found where men live together in good order and true justice. They are required too for the necessary protection of public morality. All these matters are basic to the common good and belong to what is called public order. For the rest, the principle of integrity of freedom in society should continue to be upheld.[50]

Although the term "common good" is used, it appears that, with respect to political or juridical institutions, what is at issue is only the "public order," which does *not* include the strictly "religious good" of citizens. Murray himself distinguished society's end—the common good—from the state's end—the public order:

Hence the public powers are authorized to intervene and to inhibit forms of religious expression (in public rites, teaching, observance, or behavior), only when such forms of expression seriously violate either the public peace or commonly accepted standards of public morality, or the rights of other citizens. The public powers are competent to make judgments only with regard to the essential exigencies of the public order and with regard to the necessity of legal or police intervention to protect the public order.[51]

This certainly appears to be an endorsement of religious liberty along lines that most liberals, classical and contemporary, could endorse. However, two points should be made about *Dignitatis humanae* and Fr. Murray. (1) Article 6 of *Dignitatis humanae* addresses the issue of protecting the religious liberty of "all citizens and religious communities" in situations where "because of the circumstances of a particular people, special civil recognition is given to one religious community in the constitutional organization of a State."[52] The implication seems to be, contrary to the U. S. Constitution, that some forms of religious establishmentarianism (and "favoritism") are morally licit, although in such circumstances the legitimate religious rights and liberties of minorities are to be especially scrupulously guarded. (2) The second point is that Murray apparently maintained the traditional position that 'error (including religious error) has no rights' as a *moral*, as opposed to *legal* or *juridical* (political) matter. Davies writes that

> [n]either Father Murray nor *Dignitatis humanae* so much as suggests a natural right to choose error. Father Murray specifically rejects this classic Liberal position in a footnote to his translation of *Dignitatis humanae*. He explains that to affirm that a man has a right to believe what is false or to do what is wrong is "moral nonsense". He continues: "Neither error nor evil can be the object of a right, only what is true and good."[53]

Both Murray and *Dignitatis humanae* advocate granting egalitarian *juridical* rights to what Murray regards as religious error or, more properly, to those he regards as holding erroneous religious beliefs *qua* holding such beliefs. It is possible to justify this advocacy of juridical rights in the absence of corresponding moral rights in terms of the traditional doctrine of toleration (here, moral toleration) of what cannot be claimed as a matter of *moral* right in terms of the 'pragmatic' considerations of gaining a greater good or avoiding a worse evil. Such an interpretation would indeed mean that the teaching of *Dignitatis humanae* represents a continutity with and development of—in the words of the introduction to *Dignitatis humanae*—the "traditional Catholic teaching on the moral duty of individuals and societies towards the true religion and the one Church of Christ."[54] However, in opposition to such an interpretation, Article 2 of *Dignitatis humanae* locates the "right to religious freedom" ("even in those who do not live up to their obligation of seeking the truth and adhering to it") in "the very dignity of the human person as known through the revealed word of God and by reason itself."[55]

To return to neo-natural law theory, theorists such as Grisez, Finnis, and George appear to go beyond the explicit doctrine of *Dignitatis humanae* in locating that aspect of the "dignity of the human person" that is relevant to religious liberty in 'generic' religiosity as a form of basic human good. This good is, as we saw, the good of addressing, for oneself, the 'Fundamental Option' with respect to an ultimate, transcendent reality. This good of religiosity is, *qua* basic form of human good, quite independent of religious/theological doctrine and, more gen-

erally, the good of its exercise appears to be independent of
how it is exercised so long as the particular form of its exercise
does not seriously jeopardize some other basic human good.
From the perspective of natural law, the particular form of the
exercise of the good of religiosity is good only as an instantiation of the 'generic' good of religion.

George notes that such a conception of the good of religion
will not be universally acceptable:

> People who believe, as a matter of revelation, that no participa-
> tion in the good of religion, considered as a natural human good,
> has any real value unless it is formally within the context of di-
> vinely ordained religious institutions or in line with true religious
> teachings, will reject my view on theological grounds.[56]

The view will also be rejected by those who hold that the basis of whatever degree of good there may be in diverse forms
of "participation in the good of religion" derives from the degree to which these forms of religiosity manifest or participate
in religious truth. According to such a view, the good of diverse forms of religious observance does *not* derive from such
forms' instantiation of a supposed generic human good of religiosity, as seems to be the case for neo-natural law theorists.
Hence, St. Thomas locates a reason for tolerating Jewish rites
in the fact that in them, "the truth of the faith that we hold
is prefigured."[57] However, he continues, "the rites of other un-
believers, which bear nothing of truth or of usefulness, are
not at all to be tolerated, unless perhaps so that some evil be
avoided: e.g., for avoiding scandal or divisiveness that might
come to pass from [not tolerating such rites], or for avoiding the impediment to the salvation of those who, if thus tolerated, might gradually be converted to the faith."[58]

This traditional interpretation of the derivative or mediated
value of expressions of religiosity not in conformity with
the Catholic faith also is suggested by Catholic teaching, pre-
and post-Vatican II, concerning the "many elements of sanctification and of truth [that] are found outside [the Roman Catholic Church's] visible confines."[59] According to the explication of
the doctrine *"extra ecclesiam nulla salus est"* ("there is no salvation outside the Church") contained in the recent *Catechism of
the Catholic Church*:

How are we to understand this affirmation, often repeated by the Church Fathers? Reformulated positively, it means that all salvation comes from Christ the Head through the Church which is his Body.[60]

The Church of Christ is fully subsistent in (*subsistit in*) the *Sancta (Catholica apostolica) Romana Ecclesia*, according to the teaching of Vatican II.[61] Those "many elements of sanctification and of truth" existing outside the Church owe their religious value (as a "human good") to their reflection of and participation in the fullness of sanctification and grace present in the Church. As glossed by Bernard Häring (in his orthodox days of *The Law of Christ*), this doctrine entails that "[w]herever outside the visible circle of the Catholic Church a true and salutary conversion takes place, it is granted by Christ with reference to His Church."[62] And,

> [c]ertain as all this may be, it is not to deny that also outside the bounds of the visible community of the Catholic Church there are true disciples of Christ and humble adorers of the triune God. But everywhere, where God is worshiped in spirit and truth a mysterious bond of fellowship with the "priestly people of God" of the true Church has been formed through the saving grace of God and the assent of man. . . .
> Even the Christians separated from the Church owe the treasure of doctrine which they cherish not to the book but to the Church in which the sacred scripture is ever a living source. . . .
> Nowhere except in the living visible Church—through obedient faith in her teaching, humble participation in her sacred mysteries, and imitation of her saints—are we on the sure way of the imitation of Christ.[63]

The principal theme of Robert George's *Making Men Moral* is to argue for the 'in principle' licitness of 'morals legislation', although he allows that there may well be compelling competing reasons, often of a prudential or pragmatic character, that would preclude much of such legislation. He rejects, however, an analogous position with respect to 'religious legislation'. According to Joseph R. Reisert's characterization of George's view,

> [t]hat belief may not be compelled follows from its nature: it is an "interior act," performed freely or not at all. Likewise, religious

observances may not be coerced because they, too, must be willed freely to be genuinely *religious* observances. In this way, religious and moral acts are alike: no one can be religious or moral without choosing to be so. As suggested above, George defends morals laws by noting that while coercion cannot make people moral, it may help them to become so by preventing them "from habituating themselves to corrupting vices." Although George rejects this contention, an argument parallel to his can justify religious coercion; indeed, Saint Augustine presents such an argument in a letter to the Donatist bishop of Cartennae, Vincentius.[64]

The reason George rejects the analogy between the 'in principle' licitness of morals and of religious legislation must derive from the peculiar neo-natural law conception of the basic human good of religion as an opportunity to address the 'Fundamental Option'. The goodness of this activity, *qua good of religion*, is quite independent of religious or theological content or any consideration of the truth of falsity, adequacy or inadequacy, of an individual's approach to the 'Fundamental Option' (within the bounds of public order, of course).

This attitude has much more in common with Enlightenment and post-Enlightenment, secularized conceptions of the relation of religion to the public, political sphere than it does with more traditional paleo-natural law conceptions of natural law concerning the place of religion in public life. It is also congenial to those who—unlike the neo-natural law theorists themselves—*do* think that what is important about religion is not the discernment of religious/theological truth (and consequent practice in conformity with that truth) but, rather, simply religious reflection and observance itself, whatever the content of that reflection and observance. A colleague, who is well attuned to the current American intellectual scene, assures me that many 'religious' persons in this country who are members of the cultural and socioeconomic elites take such a view of religion—as analogous to aesthetic or recreational activity, perhaps sharing the view of A. N. Whitehead that religion "is what we do with our solitude."[65] Furthermore, neo-natural law theory shares with various secular forms of liberalism the effect of separating the realm of morality as much as possible from that of religious *doctrine* and theological *content*. By way of adopting this stance, the neo-natural law tradition advances a stronger doctrine of the independence of morality from religious/theological truth than does paleo-natural law theory, which certainly recognizes a distinction between matters that are known only through revelation and (moral) matters that can be discerned by the 'natural light of reason' unaided by special revelation. This traditional distinction does not entail, however, that the moral perspective of natural law can or should prescind from a theistic or even Christian or Catholic theological orientation. On the contrary, a common attitude associated with the paleo-natural law tradition, which I myself should want largely to affirm, is well summarized by Häring:

> Moral theology, true to its own traditional principles, never has presented the virtue of religion as moral in the sense of exclusively moral. There never was the slightest connotation of such pure morality as was inaugurated by the divorce of the moral from the religious (in humanism), a divorce which was aggravated by the so-called autonomous morality (Kant), and completed by the modern ethical morality which combated and suppressed religion and sought to supplant it altogether. Unfortunately the wide-spread influence of this baneful attitude in modern times penetrated even into Catholic circles.
>
> According to the Christian teaching morality is not separate from religion. Nor can it be characterized as having perspective and motivation directed to man alone rather than to God. On the contrary, true morality may be said to accept all earthly tasks only in the relation to God . . . For the religious man morality is a summons issuing from the immediate encounter with God. It is a call for action in the world. It is not merely a task commanded by God but a task which must be ordered entirely to the glory of God.[66]

Yet, even in the absence of such a religious orientation of man's moral life, it is difficult to deny that the recognition and pursuit of the human goods specified by neo-natural law theorists according to the principles of rational morality specified by them is superior to the absence of such recognition and practice. Analogously, a political theory and system that recognizes the importance of addressing the 'Fundamental Option', a theory and regime that gives *some* assistance to citizens in 'privately' raising and addressing religious issues even while maintaining the political stance of religious indifferentism/ neutrality, would generally seem to be superior to a political theory and regime forthrightly hostile to religion. However, natural law theory that is metaphysically decontextualized has lost something important—indeed, something important by way of intellectual support and rational appeal. Also, the limitation of public, political concern to a conception of the good of religion divorced from issues of religious truth seems less than ideal. For one thing, both Marxist theory and recent experience in Western constitutional democracies (at least the American one) suggest that it is difficult to maintain a supportive public, political stance toward 'religion' on the basis of advancing the good of 'generic' religion. The viability—and vigor—of religion is, in the concrete, very much tied to the viability and strength of particular religious *traditions*. Helping to sustain the vigor of religion in public life, then, will usually depend on helping to sustain the vigor of some concrete tradition—a task that hardly seems capable of being conceptualized as a 'neutral' matter.[67]

Complete Communities, Public Squares, and Civic Souls

Aristotle's well-known characterization of the *polis* or Greek city-state as the perfect or complete (*teleios*) form of human association delineates it as a form of association that has attained the "limit of self-sufficiency" and—although it may have come into existence for the sake of securing the life of its citizens—"exists for the sake of living well."[68] Along similar lines, John Finnis speaks of various associations of human beings (e.g., family, friendships, economic, cultural, sporting associations), important though they are, as constituting "an incomplete basis for ample well-being":

> So there emerges the desirability of a 'complete community', an all-round association in which would be coordinated the initiatives and activities of individuals, of families, and of the vast network of intermediate associations. The point of this all-round association would be to secure the whole ensemble of material and other conditions, including forms of collaboration, that tend to favour, facilitate, and foster the realization by each individual of his or her personal development. . . .
> Such an ensemble of conditions includes some co-ordination (at least the negative co-ordination of establishing restraints against

interferences) of any and every individual life-plan and any and every form of association. So there is no aspect of human affairs that as such is outside the range of such a complete community.[69]

Finnis proceeds to suggest that, with respect to the modern nation-state, "[i]ts legal claims are founded, as I suggested, on its self-interpretation as a complete and self-sufficient community" (147–48). He speculates, however, that perhaps it might happen that "the good of individuals can only be fully secured and realized in the contexts of international community" (150); and if so, the claim of nation-states to be a complete community could not be fully sustained.

There are several notions rolled into the idea of a complete community. One is the notion of legal or juridical supremacy: the organization or institution that has (or claims to have) ultimate legal or juridical authority with respect to regulating the individual, reciprocal, and collective behavior of a certain group of human beings. It is clear that, despite the existence of such organizations as the United Nations and World Court, such legal or juridical authority still rests largely with nation-states. The second notion is that of ultimate sufficiency for providing all that humans need, economically, intellectually, culturally, and so forth, for both living and living well (in the manner that they choose). Such artifacts of contemporary (Western) life as the global economy, the transnational character of modern technology and knowledge (scientific and otherwise), and transnational cultural and religious movements certainly suggest that the modern nation-state is not 'complete' in this sense. Finally, there is the Aristotelian notion of self-sufficiency and completeness: the idea is that there is or should be some particular form of human association within which the distinctive human functions that constitute 'living well' (*to eu zēn*) can be most fully and perfectly exercised—an association that provides, to quote Finnis, the "co-ordination . . . of any and every individual life-plan and any and every form of association" (148).

It is so obvious that contemporary constitutional democracies, and modern nation-states in general, are ill suited for supplying 'community' in this last, Aristotelian sense that no extended argument is required here. The notion of polity as providing 'complete community' in this sense especially suggests the presence of a political soul, spirit, or 'public political culture'—a more-or-less determinate set of political institutions, principles, and attitudes—worthy and perhaps in need of justification and legitimation by means of political theory. Such a theory would also, ideally, help to stop History by stabilizing/entrenching the corporate embodiment of this political soul or spirit. This attitude makes some sense with respect to polity conceived as complete community in the Aristotelian sense, although it is certainly not beyond dispute even there.

It does not make much sense, however, with respect to such contemporary Western constitutional democracies as that of the United States. Such forms of polity simply do not even come close to instantiating the Aristotelian conception of complete community. For one thing, they are simply too large and unwieldy to fulfill such a function in the lives of individual persons. For another, as liberal political theorists have generally realized, their constituency is too heterogenous—intellectually, culturally, religiously, and in most other respects. As we have seen, liberal historiography postulates the basic shape of contemporary liberal constitutional democracies as ultimately derived from post-Reformation acquiescence, compromise, and consensus, where is has proved possible. Although this historical picture involves some oversimplification and distortion, there is a sizable element of truth to it, as there is to the claim of many contemporary theorists of political liberalism that pluralism (with respect to comprehensive conceptions of the good) constitutes an important, fixed, and apparently ineliminable feature of contemporary liberal constitutional democracies.

Yet, as I have previously suggested, contemporary theorists of political liberalism have generally not fully appreciated the force of these points. They have persisted in attempting to legitimate the soul or spirit of the contemporary liberal state (and thereby to stop History) by the development of a justificatory political theory that is 'public' in the sense that I have discussed. This political soul or spirit—this 'public political culture' that is to be theoretically represented, justified, and legitimated—is an entirely secular spirit, according to the liberal view. It must be something like a manifestation of Rawlsian public reason (rationality and reasonableness) that is not dependent upon and, in fact, can be appropriately isolated from, conceptions of the "good" current in society. But the construction of such a political theory will utilize certain theoretical assumptions and maneuvers—preeminently, some separation of the "right" and the "good"—that are quite controversial. Or it will appeal to secular, liberal perfectionist principles that are also eminently controversial. Either way, the neutrality that is supposed, in the view of theorists of political liberalism, to be characteristic of a *public* justificatory theory is compromised. And such a theorist finds herself or himself with the peculiar and futile task of attempting publicly to justify and to legitimate, to stabilize and to entrench what is relatively less controversial by the relatively more controversial: a set of political accommodations that has developed through a complex social history of maneuver, struggle, compromise, and acquiescence by a liberal political theory, which will appeal to fundamental assumptions inconsistent with many philosophical, moral, and religious convictions current—for better or worse—in the modern world.

One way of viewing the engagement of liberal theory by neo-natural law theorists is as an extended argument concerning how much and what sort of morality can be infused into or is implicitly present in the political soul—or, using a different metaphor, an argument concerning just how much of a 'complete' community the state is or should be. But both traditions agree, after a fashion, that the political soul of the political community should be a nonsectarian soul, in the religious sense of "non-sectarian." Other voices, however, have questioned the assumption of the necessity of a religiously nonsectarian soul. Richard John Neuhaus, for example, has here invoked the image of the "naked public square":

> Politics and religion are different enterprises, and it is understandable that many people would like to keep them as separate as possible. But they are constantly coupling and getting quite mixed up with one another. There is nothing new about this. It seems likely that it has always been the case in all societies.
>
> What is relatively new is the naked public square. The naked public square is the result of political doctrine and practice that would exclude religion and religiously grounded values from the conduct of public business. The doctrine is that America is a secular society. It finds dogmatic expression in the ideology of secularism. I will argue that the doctrine is demonstrably false and the dogma exceedingly dangerous.[70]

In Neuhaus's nuanced discussion there is, on the one hand, the recognition that the nature of religious influence in political matters has been—and perhaps essentially is—sectarian and particularist in nature: He maintains that "[w]hen particularist religious values and the institutions that bear them are excluded, the inescapable need to make public moral judgments will result in an elite construction of a normative morality from sources and principles not democratically recognized by the society" (86).

At times, however, in religiously diverse modern states, this particularism has been attenuated by a form of religious compromise based on the quite contingent perceived coincidence of otherwise diverse religious traditions with respect to certain public issues:

> Thinking about public ethics in the American experiment has not been all of a piece. There was, on the one hand, the belief that, if all religions were reduced to their moral essentials, they were really saying the same thing. In this sense, the public ethic was seen to be derived from a religious common denominator. . . . The approach that assumed a religious common denominator, although at times painfully contrived, worked passably well for a long time [in the United States]. It worked as long as it could be safely assumed by the country's several establishments that America is essentially white Anglo-Saxon Protestant. This was the regularly declared assumption in the great common school movement of the nineteenth century (22).

To this last comment, it might be added that, although a sort of generic Protestant domination of the public school system was for a long time a workable political compromise in the United States, it effectively excluded Roman Catholics and led to the formation of the country's elaborate parallel system of parochial elementary and secondary schools and Catholic colleges. Catholics acquiesced in this situation, no doubt largely out of political necessity, but to their benefit, some would say; and there was not, as far as I am aware, any very grave breach of public order as a result. From the Catholic and some secular perspectives this situation was far from being perfectly just. However, it is not clear that either most Catholics or most Protestants would have preferred an entirely secularized, religiously 'neutral' system of public education—although some Catholics and Protestants, as well as those without religious commitments, doubtless would have so preferred. A moral is that a political compromise, even a religiously based one, need not be entirely inclusive in order to be politically workable.

Neuhaus also recognizes that many political decisions, including some fundamental ones, in contemporary constitutional democracies rest on compromises and acquiescence that can be strained and broken in pursuit of some coherent and comprehensive *public* justifying/legitimating theory:

> In a democracy some issues are best fudged, some questions cannot be pursued relentlessly to their logical end, except at the price of imperiling public discourse. Restraint and compromise are not dirty words. . . . The fudging we have in mind need not be, indeed it must not be, deception. It is rather a readiness to patch things together that may not quite exactly fit, to live with a few loose ends not tucked in. Forgiving is not forgetting, to be sure, but in everyday life forgiving includes an element of fudging.
>
> People who compromise in accordance with the discipline of the democratic process know that they are compromising. That is, they do not tell themselves or others that it does not matter, that there was no principle at stake, that there was not a reasoning that had been stopped short of its logical end. . . . Compromise and forgiveness arise from the fact that we are imperfect creatures in an imperfect world. Democracy is the product not of a vision of perfection but of the knowledge of imperfection. In this view, compromise is not an immoral act, nor is it an amoral act. That is, the one who compromises does not step out of her role as a moral actor. To the contrary, the person who makes a compromise is making a moral judgment about what is to be done when moral judgments are in conflict (114).

Well said, indeed. One might add that, in contemporary constitutional democracies, the only truly *public* justification for many political institutions, principles, and attitudes is the fact that they devolve from workable political compromises and acquiescences, which are often quite unsystematic, piecemeal, and particularist.

Yet, at least when he wrote *The Naked Public Square*, Neuhaus seems to have retained a certain affection for a public, political soul or spirit, one that would have a religious character but would yet eschew the sectarian somewhat the manner of the secular liberal soul or spirit, e.g., the Rawlsian 'public

political culture' of a contemporary Western constitutional democracy. Neuhaus's religiously tinged public culture seems *not*
to be simply a hoped-for, contingent, historically conditioned
consensus—similar to the moral/religious "common denomina-
tor" that was once supplied in the United States by Mainstream
Anglo-Saxon Protestantism. Rather, it appears to be a desideratum that we must somehow, as a society, construct:

> A dilemma, both political and theological, facing the religious new
> right is simply this: *it wants to enter the political arena making pub-*
> *lic claims on the basis of·private truths.*The integrity of politics itself
> requires that such a proposal be resisted. Public discussions must
> be made by arguments that are public in character. A public argu-
> ment is transsubjective. It is not derived from sources of reve-
> lation or disposition that are essentially private and arbitrary. . . .
> . . . . the religious new right takes a leaf from the manual of an
> earlier Christian liberalism: the claim is made that, despite differ-
> ences in religious belief, there is a core consensus on what is moral.
> This is the much discussed "moral agenda" on which, presum-
> ably, Christians of all stripes and even nonbelievers can come to-
> gether. This approach will not wash now, however, just as it did
> not wash for long when employed by earlier religious actors in
> the public arena. The issues facing our society engage ultimacies.
> The issues themselves may be penultimate or less, but their reso-
> lution requires a publicly discussable sense of more ultimate truths
> that serve as the points of reference in guiding agreements and
> disagreements. Such resolution requires a public ethic that we do
> not now possess (36–37).

Elsewhere Neuhaus speaks of the need of "various religious
leaderships to liberate themselves from their captivity to political partisanships" and of religion's "ability to help construct
a 'sacred canopy' for the American experiment" (60). He also
writes of "true civility" as yielding "a vision of *civitas*," of the
"language of communal meaning" (61), and of an apparently
desirable "public philosophy that is democratically legitimate"
(140).

It is not clear to me that this element of Neuhaus's thought
is entirely consistent with his recognition that, under the normal assumptions concerning pluralism in contemporary constitutional democracies, political processes involve the interaction
of citizens' religious, philosophical, and moral commitments
that are particularist and, often incommensurable, particularly

at the level of ultimacies. As he himself puts it, "democracy assumes the lively interaction among people who are acting from values that are, in most instances, grounded in specific religious belief" (120). Whether or not such beliefs are religious, the "specific" seems to be crucial; and the more specific such beliefs are, the less plausible it is to see them as being fitted into any meaningful public ethic.

Nonetheless, there seems to be some attraction on Neuhaus's part—as well as on the part of other proponents of the concept of a public theology—to the idea, at least as an *ideal*, of a public, political soul or spirit, religious but 'nonsectarian' in character, to be represented by a theory (a public ethic or public theology), which all reasonably rational and decent (nonfanatical) citizens should be able to buy into. Expressed at a sufficiently high level of generality, the idea is not at all dissimilar to that of many contemporary liberal (as well as neo-natural law) theorists. Significantly, there is much disagreement concerning the shape of such a public soul and the 'theory', the public ethics or theology, that is supposed to manifest, guide, and stabilize it. This attitude in large part derives from the ideal of a complete community. The degree to which such a complete community is or might be instantiated in the political unit of a contemporary nation-state is a matter concerning which political theorists disagree. Some see complete communities, in the strong, Aristotelian sense of the term, already implicitly present in contemporary, liberal constitutional democracies of the West: it only takes the right political theory to manifest them and the correct application of public reason to polish them to a full lustre. Others, perhaps including Neuhaus, seem to regard the political instantiation of a complete community rather wistfully and perhaps a bit skeptically—as a sort of pious hope that could easily go seriously wrong.

The conviction that the political unit, more particularly, the contemporary nation-state, should go *some* way towards embodying complete community (even if 'imperfectly') is widespread. Many of us, irrespective of our political stripe (or religious, philosophical, and moral commitments), have found occasion to lament the meretricious shallowness and 'absence of principle' (by which we usually mean absence of principles that we endorse) in various aspects of contemporary public life. And for increasing numbers of urbanized, mobile citizens of contem-

porary Western nation-states there is a compartmentalization and fragmentation of social relations that may make the idea of a complete community—which would comprise the totality of our relations with others of our kind—seem a more natural or wholesome, if perhaps not altogether idyllic, way of living. However, most of us realize that no form of contemporary Western polity could possibly, or desirably, approach very close to instantiating such complete community.

The question is just how close should we expect, or wish, a contemporary constitutional democracy to come in instantiating complete community. It will by now, I hope, be obvious that the thrust of this book has been to argue that the right answer to this question is "not very close at all." I have argued that even contemporary theorists of political liberalism, with their talk of shared political culture(s) and public reason, and their search for a 'public' justifying/legitimating/entrenching/stabilizing theory, have expected and desired too much. The reader will perhaps indulge me in allowing me to refer to a political theory that assumes that an 'ensouled' complete community can, to some degree, be politically instantiated in contemporary constitutional democracies as an instance of the politics of perfection. In the absence of the politics of perfection, what do we have? The politics of imperfection. But what is that?

The Politics of Imperfection

I am well aware that this book might justly be characterized as largely critical. There is often an assumption that an author, having produced a criticism of 'competing' doctrines, thus incurs an intellectual responsibility to develop his own positive theory. In the present case, however, I have argued that the desire for a *public* justifying/legitimating (and stabilizing/entrenching) political theory is a futile desire. So I do not intend to attempt to produce such a theory as an alternative to those that have been developed by liberal, or neo-natural law, or public theology theorists. Nothing that I have said counts against the possibility or desirability of the development of a political theory *as such* or a moral theory with sociopolitical ramifications, as long as it is recognized that such theorizing will be 'partisan' in the following not necessarily pejorative sense of the term: It will appeal to fundamental principles and attitudes that there is no reason to believe will be universally, or even widely, shared by other citizens who are rational, reasonable, decent, and otherwise nondefective members of the species Homo sapiens. Indeed, I say a bit more about the place of such partisan political theorizing, from a public point of view, later in this section. I myself shall not pursue the enterprise of developing a coherent theoretical account of my own (partisan) religious-moral-political views, however, as that is not my purpose in this book.

In this section I shall sketch a conception of 'imperfect' politics—a nontheoretical, pragmatic perspective on politics. Such a conception is the only really coherent and sensible 'public' conception of politics that is possible in contemporary, liberal constitutional democracies. I do not maintain that this claim is a novel one. In fact, a number of thinkers, modern and ancient, have developed various aspects of this conception. To begin my sketch, I turn to the considerably less than positive (i.e., upbeat) comments of Alasdair MacIntyre concerning the contemporary nation-state as a complete community and the place of moral-political theory in the political life of contemporary liberal democracies. In a recently published collection of critical reflections on his work, which includes his response to these reflections, MacIntyre comments that he has been more in sympathy with liberal theorists than with their communitarian critics concerning the connection between the contemporary nation-state and community:

> Liberals however mistakenly suppose that those [totalitarian and other] evils arise from any form of political community which embodies substantive practical agreement upon some strong conception of the good. I by contrast take them to arise from the specific character of the modern nation-state, thus agreeing with liberals in this at least, that modern nation-states which masquerade as embodiments of community are always to be resisted. The modern nation-state, in whatever guise, is a dangerous and unmanageable institution, presenting itself on the one hand as a bureaucratic supplier of goods and services, which is always about to, but never actually does, give its clients value for money, and on the other as a repository of sacred values, which from time to time invites one to lay down one's life on its behalf. As I have remarked elsewhere. . . , it is like being asked to die for the telephone company.[71]

Earlier, in *After Virtue*, MacIntyre had argued that "[m]oral philosophy, as it is dominantly understood, reflects the debates and disagreements of the culture so faithfully that its controversies turn out to be unsettlable in just the way that the political and moral debates themselves are"[72]:

> What this brings out is that modern politics cannot be a matter of genuine moral consensus. And it is not. Modern politics is civil war carried on by other means. . .[73]

This obviously is eminently quotable stuff. I also believe that, with allowance for a degree of literary hyperbole, it is essentially correct. Too much focus on the hyperbole, however, may result in an unreasonably grim picture of the imperfect politics of contemporary constitutional democracies. Very few of us would choose "civil war," whether carried on by "other means" or the normal ones, as our unconditional first preference with respect to the sociopolitical framework of our lives. However, MacIntyre is correct in implying that, as long as the current pluralistic conditions obtain, it probably is the only real option for liberal, Western constitutional democracies. And, depending on exactly what the "other means" are, it may continue—at least for the time being, under the circumstances, and by and large—as a morally and politically workable option, a sociopolitical means of morally and politically "muddling along."

We contemporary, Western members of the species Homo sapiens may indeed be missing something rather important in our lack of a 'complete community'. We may even be missing something important in our lack of something purporting to be a *political* complete community in the manner of Aristotle's Greek *polis*, Rousseau's Geneva, or perhaps Jefferson's American Republic. However, most of us have become used to some of the consolations of *not* having such a political complete community. In the absence of a radical restructuring of society and without a much greater degree of cultural (religious, philosophical, moral) homogeneity than currently obtains within most of the world (particularly the more "developed" parts of it)—which homogeneity would be necessary to make feasible some version of perfect politics—we have imperfect politics. There is a sense in which this indeed is "civil war carried on by other means." According to my relatively benign interpretation, this is simply a matter of the normal nitty-gritty business of democratic politics as compromise and acquiescence, the piecemeal, contingent, and revocable formation of alliances, agreements, and modi vivendi, and the forging of consensus where we can. Except in extreme cases, which unfortunately can arise within the context of constitutional democracies just as they always have arisen in the recorded history of human relations, civil war by other means need not degenerate into civil wars by the normal means. I conclude with a series of comments, partly culled from a number of disparate sources, concerning imperfect politics. This, I fear, is as much "positive" political doctrine as the reader will find in this book.

The invocation of justificatory theory is (generally) of little use in achieving consensus in contemporary democracies. I have maintained that the attempt to rationalize, theoretically, sociopolitical compromise and agreement within the context of value-diversity that obtains in most contemporary Western democracies typically involves asking citizens to agree to more, often at a deeper and more substantive level of principle, than is contained in the agreements themselves. This is my gloss on Neuhaus's comment that "[i]n a democracy some issues are best fudged" and "cannot be pursued relentlessly to their logical end, except at the price of imperiling public discourse."[74] In contemporary democracies, the only public justification for much of the political process and its output is its political workability.

The move to a deeper level of principle in the public, political forum can often be counter-productive. This seems to me to have been the case with respect to the U.S. Supreme Court abortion decision *Roe v. Wade.* For most of us who stand in strong moral opposition to abortion, the nature of that opposition makes the issue a very difficult or impossible one on which to reach political compromise. Nonetheless, by casting abortion into the penumbra of a supposed constitutional right (to privacy), *Roe v. Wade* "upped the political (and moral) ante" in a way that was bound to result in a hardened and more militant opposition. The decision certainly did *not* supply the sort of principled rationale for abortion on demand that could serve as the theoretical basis for forging widespread public consensus on the issue. Regarding a different current American social concern—prayer in the public schools—proposals for a consti-

tutional amendment permitting (or mandating) it would be similarly counterproductive from a political point of view.

I emphasize that this eschewal of a public moral-political
theory does not entail an amoral or relativist conception of
Realpolitik. Nor does it necessarily commit one to a moral theory or a sociopolitical component of moral theory that is entirely consequentialist, utilitarian, or proportionalist. However,
it may be that consequentialist considerations may properly
figure rather more largely in action at the public level in a
contemporary pluralistic democracy than they would in one's
"private" behavior and other associational relations. For example, toleration of prostitution at the public level need not lead
to a 'toleration' of it, for consequentialist reasons, with respect
to one's own behavior or that of one's spouse. In this regard,
Stuart Hampshire argues that the assumption of a political role,
within a context of imperfect politics of contemporary constitutional democracies, carries with it

> not only new responsibilities, but a new kind of responsibility,
> which entails, first, accountability to one's followers; secondly,
> policies that are to be justified principally by their eventual con-
> sequences; and, thirdly, a withholding of some of the scruples that
> in private life would prohibit one from using people as a means
> to an end and also from using force and deceit.[75]

If all this is admitted to be true—and I am not altogether convinced that it is—one gains additional sympathy with what
Neuhaus terms the "sectarian option," in which persons (such
as the Amish), "[r]ecognizing that they cannot live out what
they believe to be the divine will in a world so severely compromised, . . . become a people apart": "The sectarian option,
seriously pursued, is one honorable alternative to the politics
of compromise."[76]

For the majority of persons who do not pursue the sectarian
option in Neuhaus's sense, there is still public value to
the development of a philosophical-moral-religious political
theory that is partisan or sectarian, in my nonpejorative sense
of these terms. Thoughtful engagement with theory that is partisan or sectarian in this sense (which, I have argued all such
theory in contemporary Western constitutional democracies will
be) can help us better to understand what can and cannot be

compromised and to what degree and in what way. Within such democratic contexts, a good part of prudence and of public civility is developing an informed sense of when one must "go to the mat" politically and when one should not.

Something less than consensus is sufficient for political workability (and legitimacy) in contemporary constitutional democracies. Nicholas Rescher has argued quite cogently that in contemporary democracies the most that we generally can hope for (and, in fact, the most that we should generally desire) is *acquiescence* as opposed to *consensus.*[77] "The crucial fact about *acquiescence,*" he contends, "is that it is generally rooted not in *agreement* with others but rather in a preparedness to get on without it" (166). Rescher would even distinguish acquiescence from compromise:

> Like compromise, acquiescence involves acceptance of an alternative which the parties involved see as suboptimal. But compromise involves (1) some sort of explicit effort at reaching a mutual accommodation, whereas acquiescence can be quite passive, and (2) compromise generally involves seeking out and adopting the best available mutually acceptable arrangement, whereas the parties involved may well acquiesce in something inferior though still tolerable (167–68).

Rescher readily admits that "acquiescence can be bad": It can be "forced or compelled" and "is no automatic route to political legitimacy." But, as he says, the same is true for consensus, because "[w]e are always entitled to ask why people agree: is it for good and valid reasons?" (175). According to Rescher, contenting ourselves with a reasonably noncoerced acquiescence is the price of the 'pluralism' characteristic of contemporary Western democracies:

> Agreeing neither in opinions nor in ends (goals, objectives, values), people can nevertheless be led to go along with the disapproval or diversity of others through a realistic realization that, in the circumstances, the cost of working to redirect their thinking into the paths of agreement is simply too high (179).

The upshot is that what Rescher calls the "polity of pluralism" (in essence, what I have termed "imperfect politics") "abandons the goal of a monolithically unified 'rational order' for the 'creative diversity' of a situation of rivalry and compe-

tition" (187). This perspective "accepts without regret the dis-
sensus of a restrained rivalry among discordant and incompatible positions none of which is able to prevail over the rest"
(189). This seems to be MacIntyre's "civil war carried on by
other means" from a more 'celebratory' point of view. Rescher,
in fact, comes close to making a virtue out of what I would
regard, simply, as necessities attaching to the contemporary
Western, democratic form of polity. No doubt there are absolutely better ways to live out our sociopolitical lives. Most of
us, however, either do not have other real options or judge the
cost of trying to bring about such options as too high.
Churchill's famous aphorism about democracy being the worst
possible form of government, except for all the others that have
been tried, is (in the words that Jeremy Bentham used on an
earlier and quite different occasion) nonsense on stilts. But, it
may be the case that under widely prevalent current social conditions, it is the best we can do in the circumstances.

In contemporary Western democracies, there is more scope for con-
sensus (or, at least, relatively stable acquiescence) with respect to
procedural elements of democratic polity than with respect to sub-
stantive political principles. In a review of Rawls's *Political Liber-*
alism, Stuart Hampshire argues—as I have done in this book—
that a political liberal in the manner of Rawls "leaves space
for the plurality of moral views to be found in any [contempo-
rary Western?] society, but only if they can be called reasonable, and this means as judged by the traditional standards of
liberalism itself."[78] In other words, the sort of neutrality to
which many theorists of political liberalism are committed by
their justifying/legitimating theory is not a real neutrality; nor
can one expect its more substantive parts to be endorsed by a
real consensus—or perhaps even acquiescence. Hampshire is
correct in suggesting that the prospects are better for many of
the more procedural aspects of contemporary democracies. A
fairly widespread endorsement, for the foreseeable future, is
perhaps possible for democratic "institutions for adversarial
argument, and equal access to them, accepted manners in ne-
gotiation, and entrenched rules and habits of advocacy, a full
ritualization of public conflicts."[79] I should maintain, however,
that moral commitment even to what is procedural in democratic polity is properly viewed as a contingent, pragmatic and
prudential commitment. It is doubtful that History can be for-

ever stopped even with respect to these procedural elements of democratic polity by any sort of justifying/legitimating theory. Nor is it clear that, under any or every imaginable set of cultural and social conditions, History *should* be thus stopped.

In conclusion, I should like briefly to invoke St. Augustine as patron of imperfect politics. Although Augustine has not received explicit attention in this book, in some sense he is its tutelary spirit. Much of the book's content owes its beginning to reflection on a comment by the scholar R. A. Markus concerning St. Augustine's mature political thought:

> The main lines of his thinking about history, society and human institutions in general (the *saeculum*) point towards a political order to which we may not unreasonably apply the anachronistic epithet 'pluralist', in that it is neutral in respect of ultimate beliefs and values.[80]

Markus proceeds to apply a sort of liberal gloss to this assessment:

> Augustine's attack on the 'sacral' conception of the Empire liberated the Roman state, and by implication, all politics, from the direct hegemony of the sacred. Society became intrinsically 'secular' in the sense that it is not as such committed to any particular ultimate loyalty. . . . His 'secularization' of the realm of politics implies a pluralistic, religiously neutral civil community. Historically, of course, such a society lay entirely beyond the horizons of Augustine's world. After centuries of development it has begun to grow from the soil of what has been Western Christendom; but it is still far from securely established in the modern world. It is assailed from many sides. Even Christians have not generally learned to welcome the disintegration of a 'Christian society' as a profound liberation for the Gospel. Augustinian theology should at least undermine Christian opposition to an open, pluralist, secular society.[81]

As I argued in an earlier essay,[82] despite the fact that there is a sense in which, according to Augustine's mature view, the political order is "neutral [or, perhaps more accurately, divided] in respect to ultimate beliefs and values," it is clear that Augustine was no liberal. It is difficult to think of anyone less likely "to welcome the disintegration of 'Christian society' as a profound liberation for the Gospel" or to celebrate the sup-

posed virtues of "an open, pluralist, secular society." Of course,
Augustine sees the value-pluralism of the *saeculum*, which is
his version of *Weltgeschichte* (comprehending all the limited,
temporal, history of humankind, including its sociopolitical
relations), as an empirical manifestation of the essential imperfection of human existence in the *saeculum*. Rather than working out anything like a theory of political legitimacy, he
inculcates a pragmatic attitude toward the *use* of political means
for attaining higher and ultimately spiritual ends, an attitude
that is on a par with his attitude toward the use of all temporal goods. As I argued earlier, it is consistent with such an attitude toward political means that, in some social contexts, "it
is politically expedient to deal with such diversity in much the
way that the modern liberal state does."[83] But such toleration
is not a matter of liberal principle:

> Like all institutions of the *saeculum*, political authority is to *used
> (utendum)* by citizens of the *civitas peregrina* [foreign city], as cir-
> cumstances permit, to further the ends of the heavenly city, which
> of course are their own proper ends. But the details of such use
> can, it seems, greatly depend upon various contingencies: what is
> an appropriate use in one set of circumstances may not be appro-
> priate in other circumstances. Consequently, there is nothing in
> principle in Augustine's political thought to rule out the use of
> political coercion, such as he came to advocate with respect to the
> Donatist schismatics. Of course, there is also nothing in his ma-
> ture thought that, as a matter of general political principle, *en-
> joins* such a use of political authority. Consequently, it is not
> surprising to find Augustine discussing the advisability of coer-
> cion in pastoral, theological, scriptural, psychological, and practi-
> cal terms. Strictly *political* considerations, considerations phrased
> in terms of 'human' or political rights, liberties, etc., of the sort
> that would invariably be raised in modern discussions simply do
> not occur.[84]

There is a sense in which, for Augustine, History is already
stopped in the *saeculum* because it is not really going anywhere:
the eschatological end of human beings represents a discontinu-
ity with *Weltgeschichte*, which, in Augustine's mature view, is
essentially non-developmental. Although there may be great
variations in its social, political, cultural, and economic institutions, these should not be of ultimate concern to humans

and do not constitute any sort of teleological pattern. Ernest L. Fortin speaks perceptively of Augustine's "lack of interest in politics":

> If Augustine can be said to have any concern for politics at all, it is not for its own sake but because of the moral problems that it poses for Christians who, as citizens, are willy-nilly caught up in it. These problems have their common root in the nature of Christianity itself, which is essentially a nonpolitical religion. Unlike Judaism and Islam, the two other great monotheistic religions of the West, it does not call for the formation of a separate community or provide a code of laws by which that community might be governed. It takes for granted that its followers will continue to live as full-fledged citizens of the political society to which they belong and share its way of life as long as they are not forced to indulge in practices that are directly at odds with their basic beliefs, as were, for example, idolatry and emperor worship.[85]

Such an interpretation of Christianity has been and will continue to be controversial. There is no doubt, however, that it represents an important and continuing tradition in Christian sociopolitical thought according to which, in the words of Neuhaus, Christianity offers "no coherent, detailed, revealed design for the social order."[86] This does not mean Christianity must dispense with moral injunctions having sociopolitical implications or that it is somehow at fault (e.g., violating the demands of civility) for importing such partisan considerations into the public square. It certainly does not mean that Christianity need be committed, as a matter of principle, to a pluralist, secular political order—an order that is to be justified/legitimated by a theory supposedly free from the taint of partisan religious, philosophical, or moral convictions.

What this "Augustinian" attitude does suggest is the appropriateness of a certain flexibility and adaptability with respect to the political order and a prudential recognition of the inherent limitations of political solutions to human problems. As Fortin puts it,

> Augustine never called for the extrusion of ethics [including, of course, religiously-based ethics] from the realm of politics; but neither did he ever dream that the two realms could be simply identified.

It follows that for Augustine the notion of a Christian polity . . . is at best a comforting and at worst a fatal illusion, possibly leading to fanaticism, as it often has over the centuries. Christian wisdom and political power are not only distinct but always more or less at odds with each other in accordance with the vicissitudes of history and the inclinations of our "restless hearts." Some regimes are obviously superior to others but nothing suggests that any of them will ever be able to fulfill our deepest longings. Christianity as Augustine understands it does indeed supply a solution to the problem of human life, but it is not a solution that is attainable in and through political society.[87]

Not only does it seem, as an empirical matter, that there is little possibility of stopping History by attempting to justify/ legitimate a certain form of polity but, from the Augustinian point of view, all politics will be radically imperfect. Consequently, the enterprise of attempting to stop History at a certain political juncture is far from being the most fundamental moral imperative.

Notes

1. Richard John Neuhaus, *The Naked Public Square: Religion and Democracy in America* (Grand Rapids, Mich.: W. B. Eerdmans Publishing Co., 1984), 115.

2. See Charles Larmore, *Patterns of Moral Complexity* (Cambridge: Cambridge University Press, 1987), 55–59.

3. Rawls, *Political Liberalism*, pp. 13–14.

4. Robert P. George, *Making Men Moral: Civil Liberties and Public Morality* (Oxford: Clarendon Press, 1993), vii.

5. David Hume, *A Treatise of Human Nature*, ed., L. A. Selby-Bigge, 2nd ed. rev. by P. H. Nidditch (Oxford: Clarendon Press, 1978), bk. 1, pt. 4, sec. 7, 271–72.

6. St. Thomas Aquinas, *Summa Theologiae*, ed., P. Caramello (Turin and Rome: Marietti, 1952), I^a II^{ae}, q. 91, a. 4.

7. John Finnis, *Natural Law and Natural Rights* (Oxford: Clarendon Press, 1980), 49.

8. Aquinas, *Summa Theologiae*, I^a II^{ae}, q. 94, a. 2.

9. Russell Hittinger, *A Critique of the New Natural Law Theory* (Notre Dame, Ind.: University of Notre Dame Press, 1987), 32.

10. Finnis, *Natural Law*, 34.

11. Ibid.

12. Ibid.

13. The list of Grisez contains four "reflexive" basic human goods

and three "substantive" basic human goods. In the former category are self-integration, practical reasonableness or authenticity, justice and friendship, and religion or holiness; in the latter category are "life itself, including health, physical integrity, safety, and the handing on of life to new persons," "knowledge of various forms of truth and appreciation of various forms of beauty or excellence," and "activities of skillful work and of play" (Germain Grisez, *Christian Moral Principles*, vol. 1: *The Way of the Lord Jesus* [Chicago: Francisan Herald Press, 1983], 124–125).

    14. See Finnis, *Natural Law*, chap. 4.

    15. Ibid., 30.

    16. Ibid., 100–101.

    17. Grisez, *Christian Moral Principles*, 184.

    18. Finnis, *Natural Law*, 105.

    19. Grisez, *Christian Moral Principles*, 205.

    20. Finnis, *Natural Law*, 108.

    21. Ibid., 168.

    22. George, *Making Men Moral*, 189.

    23. Unless (a) the premise set is logically inconsistent, in which case *any* conclusion follows (b) the conclusion is a logical truth, which follows from any premise set.

    24. Hume, *Treatise*, bk. 3, pt. 1, sec. 1, 458.

    25. Ibid., bk. 2, pt. 3, sec. 3, 416.

    26. Aquinas, *Summa Theologiae*, I^a II^{ae}, q. 91, a. 2.

    27. Finnis, *Natural Law*, 35.

    28. Ibid., 36.

    29. Aquinas, *Summa Theologiae*, II^a II^{ae}, q. 110, a. 3.

    30. Ibid.

    31. Ibid.

    32. John Finnis, *Moral Absolutes: Tradition, Revision, and Truth* (Washington, D.C.: Catholic University of America Press, 1991), 85–86.

    33. Finnis, *Natural Law*, 118.

    34. Jeffrie G. Murphy, "Afterword: Constitutionalism, Moral Skepticism, and Religious Belief," in *Constitutionalism: The Philosophical Dimension*, Contributions in Legal Studies, no. 46, ed. Alan S. Rosenbaum (New York: Greenwood Press, 1988), 247.

    35. See Finnis, *Moral Absolutes*, 101ff.

    36. Hittinger, *Critique of the New Natural Law Theory*, 42–43.

    37. Ibid., 158–59.

    38. Finnis, *Natural Law*, 89.

    39. George, *Making Men Moral*, 221.

    40. It must be noted, however, that both Finnis and Grisez express reservations concerning current 'Fundamental Option' theory in theology. Grisez divides current theories of the Fundamental Option into (a) those that treat the "basic commitment" attendant on the Fundamental Option "either as an extraordinary choice or an aspect of many

choices" and (b) those that regard the "fundamental option as something more mysterious than a basic commitment: a total self-disposal,
attributed not to free choice but to another freedom, often called 'fundamental freedom' or 'basic freedom'" (Grisez, *Christian Moral Principles*, 383). Grisez himself recommends a "synthesis of [St. Thomas
Aquinas's] account and certain insights of fundamental-option theory.
The fundamental option of Christian life is the act of faith. This is not
simply an option for God or moral goodness; it has specific determina-
tions, a definite content. This commitment excludes not only sins against
faith but, implicitly, acts of any kind inconsistent with living as members of the Church" (ibid., 399).

41. For more on the problem for neo-natural law of sorting out what
Hittinger calls the "foundational" and "implicational" approaches to the
relation between religion and practical reason (particularly as manifest
in natural law), see Hittinger, *Critique of the New Natural Law Theory*,
especially chap. 4. For more, in general, on the issue of the place of
religion in a contemporary liberal state that has, in Marx's words, been
"emancipated from religion," see my "Religion and the Common Good,"
forthcoming in *The Political Left and Right, and the Common Good*, ed.
Paul W. McNellis, S.J.

42. Finnis, *Natural Law*, 389. See also Finnis, *Fundamentals of Ethics*
(Oxford: Clarendon Press, 1982), 146: "These philosophical speculations
about the character of D's existing cannot, so far as I can see, be established with philosophical certainty. But the conclusion that D exists and
is an uncaused cause can be affirmed with philosophical certainty."

43. Hittinger, *Critique of the New Natural Law Theory*, 20.

44. George, *Making Men Moral*, 220–221.

45. Ibid., 222.

46. Ibid.

47. Michael Davies, *The Second Vatican Council and Religious Liberty*
(Long Prairie, Minn.: The Neumann Press, 1992), 19.

48. More narrowly, violation of the public order is an offense that
could lead to a breach of peace.

49. Davies, *Second Vatican Council*, 120. I do not here have space to
do justice to Murray, who seems to me to have been a more subtle and
nuanced thinker than many of his critics and some of his supporters
have allowed. With respect to the issue of religious liberty, one should
surely begin with his *The Problem of Religious Freedom*, Woodstock Papers, no. 7 (Westminster, Md.: The Newman Press, 1965). But there is
much more by Murray that is relevant. And there is an abundance of
secondary source material. See the splendid recent study by Keith J.
Pavlischek, *John Courtney Murray and the Dilemma of Religious Toleration*
(Kirksville, Mo.: Thomas Jefferson University Press, 1994). Also Donald
E. Pelotte, S.S.S., *John Courtney Murray: Theologian in Conflict* (New York,
Ramsey, N.J., and Toronto: Paulist Press, 1976); Robert P. Hunt, Ken-

neth L. Grasso, eds., *John Courtney Murray and the American Civil Conversation* (Grand Rapids, Mich.: W. B. Eerdmans Publishing Co., 1992); Thomas T. Love, *John Courtney Murray: Contemporary Church-State Theory* (Garden City, N. Y.: Doubleday, 1965).

50. *Dignitatis humanae*, art. 7, trans. Laurence Ryan, in *Vatican Council II: The Conciliar and Post Conciliar Documents*, ed. Austin Flannery, O.P. (Northport, N. Y.: Costello Publishing Co., 1975), 805.

51. Murray, *The Problem of Religious Freedom*, Woodstock Papers, no. 7 (Westminster, Md.: The Newman Press, 1965). 43.

52. *Dignitatis humanae*, art. 6, 804.

53. Davies, *Second Vatican Council*, 18.

54. *Dignitatis humanae*, art. 1, 800.

55. Ibid., art. 2, 800, 801.

56. George, *Making Men Moral*, 223.

57. Aquinas, *Summa Theologiae*, II^a II^{ae}, q. 10, a. 11.

58. Ibid.

59. *Lumen gentium*, art. 8, trans. Colman O'Neill, O.P., in *Vatican Council II*, ed. Flannery, 357.

60. *Catechism of the Catholic Church.* art. 846, English trans. (Liguori, Mo.: Liguori Publications, 1994), 224.

61. *Lumen gentium*, art. 8, 357.

62. Bernard Häring, *The Law of Christ*, vol. 1 (Westminster, Md.: The Newman Press, 1961). 416.

63. Ibid., vol. 3, 157–159.

64. Joseph R. Reisert, "Legislating Morality?," *First Things: A Monthly Journal of Religion and Public Life* 43 (May 1994): 50.

65. Cited and discussed by George Parkin Grant in *English-Speaking Justice* (Notre Dame, Ind.: University of Notre Dame Press, 1985), 85.

66. Häring, *The Law of Christ*, vol. 2, 122–123.

67. "Tradition" seems to be just as important as "concrete" here. The French revolutionary attempt to invent, for sociopolitical reasons, a religion *de novo* yielded results as unsuccessful as they were ludicrous.

68. Aristotle, *Politics*, ed. and trans. Jean Aubonnet (Paris: Societe d'Edition Les Belles Lettres, 1968), 1.2.1252a27–30.

69. Finnis, *Natural Law*, 147–148.

70. Neuhaus, *The Naked Public Square*, vii.

71. John Horton and Susan Mendus, eds., *After MacIntyre: Critical Perspectives on the Work of Alasdair MacIntyre* (Cambridge and Oxford: Polity Press, 1994), 303.

72. Alasdair MacIntyre, *After Virtue: A Study in Moral Theory* (Notre Dame, Ind.: University of Notre Dame Press, 1981), 235.

73. Ibid., 236.

74. Neuhaus, *The Naked Public Square*, 114.

75. Stuart Hampshire, *Morality and Conflict* (Oxford: Basil Blackwell Publishers, 1983), 124.

76. Neuhaus, *The Naked Public Square*, 118–119.

77. Nicholas Rescher, *Pluralism: Against the Demand for Consensus* (Oxford: Clarendon Press, 1993).

78. Stuart Hampshire, "Liberalism: The New Twist," *The New York Review of Books* 40, no. 14 (August 12, 1993): 44.

79. Ibid., 46.

80. R. A. Markus, *Saeculum: History and Society in the Theology of St. Augustine* (Cambridge: Cambridge University Press, 1970), 151.

81. Ibid., 173.

82. Michael J. White, "Pluralism and Secularism in the Political Order: St. Augustine and Theoretical Liberalism," *The University of Dayton Review* 22, no. 3 (Summer 1994): 137–154.

83. Ibid., 147.

84. Ibid.

85. Ernest L. Fortin, introduction to *Augustine: Political Writings*, trans. M. W. Tkacz and D. Kries, ed. E. L. Fortin and D. Kries, with R. Gunn (Indianapolis and Cambridge, Mass.: Hackett Publishing Company, Inc., 1994), vii.

86. Neuhaus, *The Naked Public Square*, p. 120.

87. Fortin, introduction to *Augustine: Political Writings*, xxvi.

Chapter 5

Epilogue

In consideration of those readers who like to see "the arguments" in a work such as this made quite explicit, I shall attempt to spell out what I think the architectonic argument of the preceding chapters has been. It is logically equivalent to a destructive dilemma.

> Premise 1: If there is a plausible liberal 'public' political theory (of justification/legitimation and stabilization/entrenchment), then it will either (a) ultimately appeal to controversial, perfectionist assumptions concerning aspects of human life that are deserving of recognition and promotion in the political sphere or (b) rest content with spelling out, systematizing, and tidying up the actual (but apparently contingent) results of democratic processes generating consensus, compromise, or acquiescence.

> Premise 2: A plausible liberal 'public' political theory (of justification/legitimation and stabilization/entrenchment) must *not* ultimately appeal to controversial assumptions concerning aspects of human life that are deserving of recognition and promotion in the political sphere.

> Premise 3: A plausible liberal 'public' political theory (of justification/legitimation and stabilization/entrenchment) must *not* rest content with spelling out, systematizing, and tidying up the actual (but apparently contingent) results of democratic processes generating consensus, compromise, or acquiescence.

> Conclusion: It is not the case that there is plausible liberal 'public' political theory (of justification/legitimation and stabilization/entrenchment).

It does not require great philosophical subtlety or acumen to produce a valid argument. What is at issue is such an argument's soundness—the truth of its premises. The preceding chapters may be regarded as an extended argument for the plausibility of the argument's premises. I do not believe that I have produced apodictic, irrefutable, 'knock-down' arguments for the premises—that outcome, according to the usage of Lewis Carroll's Humpty Dumpty, would be designated "glory". Such glory, I suspect, is seldom found in sociopolitical theory. But I do contend that a reasonable case can be made.

Perfectionist liberalism attempts to falsify Premise 2—to make political use of some particular (controversial) comprehensive conception of the good or of some 'common ground' shared by a number (but not all) comprehensive conceptions current in society. This involves appeal to substantive principles concerning which among various human desires, goals, and commitments are worthy of political protection and support, and which are not. The problem, I have suggested, with such outright perfectionist liberalism is that it appears to be at odds with liberalism's own favored historiography. Insofar as liberalism conceives of itself as devolving from post-Reformation, Enlightenment democratic processes of compromise- and consensus-formation, it will be uneasy with a *public* theory of political justification and legitimation that appeals to controversial perfectionist assumptions—assumptions that, I have argued, are often *more* controversial than the concrete compromises, acquiescences, and consensuses that they are supposed to justify and legitimate. And it is reasonable to suppose that the better the theory is at justifying a particular liberal political agenda, the more perfectionist and controversial it will be.

There are compelling historical reasons, however, for liberalism to desire a theory of justification/legitimation to be a *public* one—a theory that, in principle, everyone can endorse. It is no surprise to find—as the theoretical crystallization of liberalism's pragmatic origins in compromise and consensus—a common liberal tradition of grounding political legitimacy in idealized universal consent, after the manner of Rousseau, Rawls, and Habermas. Thus, it is not so easy *for liberalism* to avoid the destructive dilemma by denying Premise 2. In other words, it is not so clear that, in taking the perfectionist turn, liberalism can retain its distinctively liberal identity. This identity would seem to entail commitment to the ideal of a public theory of legitimation, which ipso facto will not be a perfectionist theory that appeals to 'partisan' perfectionist assumptions.

There is also abundant support for Premise 3. A liberal public theory of justification and legitimation has as the object of its ministrations a *particular* set of liberal principles, institutions, and attitudes. Its aim is to stop History at a certain suitably idealized juncture. It does not intend, then, to justify and stabilize *any* contingent consensus, compromise, or acquiescence resulting from actual, messy democratic political processes. To deny Premise 3 would be to make political theory "democratic in the wrong way," to use Rawls's phrase.[1] It would also be to draw the normative teeth from political theory in a way that belies the idea that such a theory is supposed to be a theory of justification and legitimation.

If there are good reasons not to deny Premise 2 or Premise 3, from the perspective of a liberal political theory that is intended to be both legitimating and public, it is imperative to deny Premise 1—i.e., to avoid the exhaustive dichotomy of its consequent. Hence what I have termed the "search for a *tertium quid*." Although it seems to me that such attempts to circumvent Premise 1 represent the best sort of response that liberal theory can make to the destructive dilemma, it also seems to me—as I have argued—that the search for a *tertium quid* is ultimately futile. The search for the *tertium quid* has generally been directed either to *neutral rational justifiability* or to *tradition* and *culture*.

A continuing program of liberalism, carried on at least since Rousseau, is to find a notion of (practical) rationality or reasonableness that is thick enough to justify determinate political prescriptions and proscriptions (of a liberal stripe) but not so thick as to appeal obviously to perfectionist (and controversial) assumptions about issues of ultimate value with respect to human life, in both its individual and social aspects. Were such a notion of rationality and reasonableness to be found, it could serve as the basis of an idealized-consent or -consensus model of political legitimacy. That is, a set of liberal principles, institutions, and attitudes could be justified by appeal to what *each person should* (in an epistemic-moral sense of "should") be able to agree to, irrespective of his or her conception of what is and is not really valuable with respect to our living of our human lives. This would supply an 'objective' *tertium quid* between a forthright appeal to perfectionist considerations to justify a political agenda and the non-justification of simply accepting the contingent results of democratic processes. The problem with this program, I have maintained, is that practical reason(ableness) must begin with some assumptions if it is to produce substantive political conclusions. Too 'neutral' a conception of rational justifiability will yield too few and too thin political conclusions. To obtain anything close to what is recognizable as a determinate set of liberal political prescriptions and proscriptions, some strongly normative (i.e., perfectionist) assumptions must be tacitly presupposed. These assumptions are not always easy to see, but they are there. For example, Rawls's employment of the notions of reasonableness and public reason has the effect of prioritizing the value of social cooperation 'for its own sake' over any competing element of a citizen's comprehensive conception of the good. And I see no way of justifying such a prioritization, which, on the face of things, seems irrational, without appeal to some perfectionist considerations. So, in order to fulfill effectively its justifying/legitimating role, 'neutral rational justifiability' must shed its neutrality; but it then loses its status as *tertium quid* and slides back into the perfectionist half of the dichotomy.

The other direction in which some liberal theorists have looked in search of the *tertium quid* is that of culture or tradition. Perhaps there is enough substance to our shared social culture and traditions (e.g., Rawls's "public political culture of a democratic society"[2]) to supply the basis of a liberal theory of political justification and legitimation. There doubtless would be perfectionist elements to such a foundation of liberal justificatory theory, but at least those elements would be universally (or all-but-universally) accepted by the citizens of a society at a given time. This seems to be the Rawlsian method of reflective equilibrium writ large—i.e., transferred from individual to 'society' (at a certain time and in a certain place).

I have questioned whether—in contemporary Western constitutional democracies—there really is enough substance (beyond the procedural) to the ideas of public culture and political traditions to serve as the foundation for a political theory that is supposed to justify and legitimate a more-or-less determinate political agenda. But, apart from this point, the justification and legitimation that such a theory could provide would be a justification/legitimation *relative* to a particular culture or set of traditions (at a particular time). In other words, such 'justification' would not amount to a real *tertium quid* but would collapse into the side of the original dichotomy that amounts only to "spelling out, systematizing, and tidying up the actual (but apparently contingent) results of democratic processes generating consensus, compromise, or acquiescence."

It is difficult to see why, from the Rawlsian perspective, a political theory so conceived would not be "political in the wrong way." One suspects that such a theory could *avoid* being "political in the wrong way" (in Rawls's sense) only by smuggling into the ideas of 'public culture' and 'political traditions' elements that are perfectionist and controversial—i.e., controversial in the sense of *not* reflecting the results of democratic processes of consensus, compromise, and acquiescence.

My conclusion is that there are good reasons to think that the destructive dilemma is not only valid but sound. For reasons that should now be clear, the argument is particularly telling against the concept of a *liberal* 'public' theory of justification/legitimation. But the considerations of chapter 4 suggest that the argument is also a problem for competing theories of justification/legitimation if those theories adopt a sufficiently liberal framework of assumptions and presuppositions. The moral for nonliberal political theorists is, I think, obvious.

Notes

1. Rawls, *Political Liberalism*, 40.
2. Ibid., 13.

Index

Leo XIII, Pope, 115–16
liberal democracies. *See* constitutional (liberal) democracies
liberalism: perfectionist liberalism, 28, 32, 70, 75, 146, 157,
  178; two senses of, 107. *See
  also* classical liberalism;
  political liberalism
libertarianism, 46, 48–49, 98
liberty. *See* freedom
Locke, John, 5–10; as classical
  liberal, 107; *Epistola de Tolerantia*, 6; on equality, 47; hedonism of, 7–8; Kant compared
  with, 15, 16; on morality as
  science, 7; privatized conception of vocation, 51; on
  property, 47–48; on reciprocity,
  50; on religion as inward, 6;
  on religious toleration, 6–8,
  36n13
Luther, Martin, 18

Macedo, Stephen, 32, 33, 37n53
MacIntyre, Alasdair: on complete
  community and the nation-
  state, 163–64; on Kant, 12; on
  practical reason, 94; on
  teleological ethics, 11, 22, 24,
  40
Macpherson, C. M., 47, 48
Marcuse, Herbert, 82
Maritain, Jacques, 42, 76n7
Markus, R. A., 169
Marx, Karl, 28, 29
Marxism, 34, 82, 154
maximin strategy, 56
meaning, ultimate ground of,
  143–44
mental reservation, doctrine of, 7
Mill, John Stuart, 107
modus vivendi: egalitarian distributive justice as prudential,
  52–61; freedom of thought/

conscience as, 3; fundamental
  rights as, 3; justification for
  post-Reformation, 4; political
  liberalism as, 3–4, 56. *See also*
  compromise
money, 47–48
Montaigne, Michel de, 19
Moore, Margaret, 34
morality: intuitionism, 139–40;
  legislating, 141, 151–52;
  naturalistic fallacy, 139; natural
  law theory on foundation of,
  11; neo-natural law theory on
  principles of, 132–33; "ought"
  derived from "is," 134–39;
  political liberalism staking out
  high moral ground, 34, 75;
  public theology/ethics, ix, 161;
  and religion, 152–53; religious
  right's moral agenda, 160; as
  scientific for Locke, 7; social
  virtues, 112–13; ultimate
  ground of meaning and value,
  143–44; universalizability, 133.
  See also fundamental (basic)
  rights; good, the; justice; practical reason
moral-political theory, public. *See*
  political theory
Murphy, Jeffrie G., 65, 72, 78n41,
  78n42, 120n14, 139
Murray, John Courtney, 147, 148–
  49, 174n49

Naked Public Square, The (Neuhaus), 123, 157–61, 165, 166,
  171
nation-state, the: complete community not instantiated in, ix,
  155, 161–62, 163–64; legal
  authority remaining in, 155; a
  public culture for, viii–ix. *See
  also* constitutional (liberal)
  democracies

to provide, 30, 32, 58, 81, 83–
91, 93–95, 125, 157, 162, 177–
81; Rawl's concept as normative, 23, 84–89
state of nature, equality in, 45, 46
stopping History, 81–121; for
Augustine, 170; complete community as, 156; democratic
procedures as insufficient for,
168–69; for Marxism, 82;
moral-political theory as, vii;
no compelling reason for, ix–x;
political liberalism as desiring,
30, 58, 71, 73, 75, 81–82, 89–
91, 93, 110, 118–19, 156, 179;
political liberalism as end of
History, 28–30; political theory
for, 82, 89, 124
Stroll, Avrum, 19

telos, human, 11–12, 22–27, 40–41
tertium quid: a political conception of justice as, 86; political
liberalism seeking, 2, 32–33,
94, 179–81; practical reason as,
92, 94–95, 179–80; for Rawls,
32, 33, 109–11
Thomas Aquinas, St. *See* Aquinas,
St. Thomas
thought, freedom of. *See* freedom
of thought/conscience
tolerance, 112–19; and distributive

justice, 113–14; dogmatic intolerance, 114; of error, 114–15; as
matter of prudence, 114, 118;
traditional view of, 114–19
toleration, religious: Aquinas on,
115, 150; Leo XIII on, 115–16;
Locke on, 6–8; skepticism as
supporting, 18, 19, 20–28; traditional understanding of, 117;
Voltaire on, 18, 19. *See also*
freedom of thought/con-
science; religious freedom
Toleration Act, 6

Unger, Roberto Mangobeira, 23–
24
universal histories: Kant on, 15;
liberal Protestant orientation
of, 3–4; of political liberalism,
28
universalizability, 133

value, ultimate ground of, 143–44
Varon, François, 19
virtues, social, 112–13
volonté générale (general will), 67,
85, 90, 93
Voltaire, 18, 19

Walzer, Michael, 42–43
Whitehead, A. N., 152

About the Author

Michael J. White is professor of philosophy at Arizona State University. He is the author of *Agency and Integrality, The Continous and the Discrete, Certainty and Surface in Epistemology and Philosophical Method*, and many articles in metaphysics, ethics, and political theory.